Should it be ours to drain the cup of grieving
even to the dregs of pain, at thy command,
we will not falter, thankfully receiving
all that is given by thy loving hand.

—Dietrich Bonhoeffer
NEW YEAR (1945)

THE CUP OF GRIEF

Biblical Reflections on Sin, Suffering and Death

Roland J. Faley, T.O.R.

ALBA · HOUSE   NEW · YORK

SOCIETY OF ST. PAUL, 2187 VICTORY BLVD., STATEN ISLAND, NEW YORK 10314

Library of Congress Cataloging in Publication Data

Faley, Roland James.
The cup of grief.

Includes bibliographical references.
1. Good and evil--Biblical teaching. 2. Theodicy. I. Title.
BS680.G6F34   242'.4   77-6839
ISBN 0-8189-0352-X

Nihil Obstat:

Daniel V. Flynn, J.C.D.
Censor Librorum

Imprimatur:

✝ James P. Mahoney, D.D.
Vicar General, Archdiocese of New York
April 9, 1977

*The Nihil Obstat and Imprimatur
are a declaration that a book or pamphlet is considered
to be free from doctrinal or moral error. It is not implied that
those who have granted the Nihil Obstat and Imprimatur agree
with the contents, opinions or statements expressed.*

*Designed, printed and bound in the United States of
America by the Fathers and Brothers of the Society of St. Paul,
2187 Victory Boulevard, Staten Island, New York, 10314,
as part of their communications apostolate.*

1 2 3 4 5 6 7 8 9 (Current Printing: first digit).

To My Mother

PREFACE

There are two factors which explain the present work, both of them related to our "questioning" times. The first is the intention of considering human suffering and death in relation to a provident God. The question is neither academic nor theoretical; at some point in time it touches all of us. In this sense, the book can be said to be pastoral in its orientation. Why is it that a God who is recognized and worshipped as Goodness itself permits the tragic to mar human existence? The author makes no claims to startling new insights into a mystery which has taxed the resources of sages for centuries. What I have attempted to do is to record the expression of this problem as it emerged and developed in biblical thought, together with the evaluation that accompanied it. This is done in what I have termed "reflections," which admittedly means that I have painted with a large brush, leaving to others a more detailed analysis of texts and passages which, in their frequent complexity, would require further elaboration. In the present instance, such would only dull the cutting edge of a work which has a more specific objective. In addition, a detailed study of sin, suffering and death would have to include, in the interests of completeness, sections of the Old and New Testament literature which are not represented here.

The reader will find in this work the major trends and developments in biblical thought related to the problem of evil. What will emerge is a picture of the biblical authors wrestling with the problem no less than their modern counterparts. And if it be argued that not even God's revelation gives us a completely satisfactory solution, there is no questioning the fact that the culmination of Judeo-Christian reflection situates the problem in a new and different context. Grief is no less real for its being integrated into God's plan of salvation, but there is no doubt that such alters its meaning. It is this insight which offers consolation and hope in the shadow of a mystery that perdures.

The second purpose of the book has also a pastoral scope. It has become common in modern biblical research to speak of revelation in organic terms. An understanding of God and his relationship to creation was not given in the blinding light of immediate comprehension. It was a long, and at times tortuous process. There is no key biblical concept which did not go through a more or less lengthy period of refinement. There is no concept which did not admit of different theological approaches. Theological pluralism is an idea that enjoys broad currency today, but it is safe to say that it began when men first addressed the God-question. The Bible itself amply illustrates the point, and the problem of evil is but one striking example.

My desire to write on this subject was enhanced by extended stays in India in recent years. It was there that human anguish struck me most forcefully, coupled with the recognition that misfortune does not diminish India's sense of the divine and reverence for the sacred. It is a paradox which requires the framework of a deep religious faith to be understood. I was once again compelled to see the intimate bond that unites faith and suffering and was spurred to complete a study which had long been a latent aspiration.

No author is without indebtedness, and I unhesitatingly express my own to my fellow biblical scholars, whose research is amply represented in these pages. A special note of acknowledgment is due to my Old Testament mentors, Roland E. Murphy and Patrick W. Skehan. Whatever virtues the present work may possess are in large measure due to the standards of scholarship and integrity which they personally inspired in me. The invaluable technical assistance of Anne Udovich in preparing the manuscript for publication cannot go unmentioned.

CONTENTS

THE CUP OF GRIEF

I.

THE OLD TESTAMENT PROBLEM OF EVIL

Speculation invariably springs from experience. The "whys" and "wherefores" of philosophical inquiry are deeply rooted in man's attempt to give reason and meaning to his existence. What ancient man failed to achieve in philosophical sophistication he channeled into the realm of myth. Many of the important questions raised by philosophy on the origins of the cosmos and man, the purpose of human existence, the quest for truth and happiness, were anything but alien to the myths of antiquity, as clearly evidenced, for example, in the Mesopotamian **Gilgamesh** or **Enuma Elish.** Myth is nothing more than a human effort to express the inexpressible, to speak of the unknown in terms of the known, and it is safe to say that no culture, ancient or modern, has ever been without it. In short, ancient man, no less than his modern counterpart, was very much taken up with the "ultimate questions."

The fact that Old Testament man had experienced a revealing God did not exempt him from wrestling with many of these same "ultimate questions" nor, for that matter, from using the language of myth in speaking of Yahweh, the "wholly other," and his relations with the universe and man. To be familiar with the Old Testament is to realize that while the God of the Hebrews was a unique type of revealer, he was anything but a divine problem-solver. Indeed, Israel's experience of Yahweh raised as many questions as it solved, and none of these was more vexing than the problem of evil.

The daily experience of the Old Testament man provided its joys and its sorrows, its bliss and its grief. To live with these was one thing; to explain them, quite another. As we shall see, explaining the brighter side of life in terms of divine reward for good conduct presented problems of its own. But far more elusive of explanation, in terms of commonplace experience, were suffering, misfortune, degradation and death. They were difficult enough to endure in the concrete, but what made them insufferable in the course of Israelite history was the inability to explain the "why" behind them.

It was only the "good life" which could adequately fulfill man's deepest desires. Health, peace, family, length of days, food and drink—all receive more than their share of encomiums in the Old Testament. While it may annoy us to see a full life described in such terrestrial terms, attempts to spiritualize this worldly outlook are doomed to failure. Life is equated with possession of the promised land (Dt 4:1), prosperity (Ps 34:13), money and good wine (Qoh 10:19). Such were to be enjoyed not only because they afforded pleasure in themselves but, even more importantly, because they were the unmistakable sign of divine favor. Since such benefits were at Yahweh's disposal, they could only be showered on the man who deserved them. By the same token, misfortune was the antithesis of all this; it made life miserable, drew one closer to death and was the sign of the Lord's disfavor. Thus it weighed heavily on the Hebrew heart.

True, this question is interwoven with Old Testament anthropology, which we shall shortly consider. Our present concern is with Hebrew psychology and the extent to which the Hebrew Bible reflects the anguish of suffering. It is deeply emblazoned on the pages of the sacred text and, for the Christian reader, whose perspectives on suffering are considerably different, it is often an enigma. How can supposedly religious people be so guilty of antagonism toward the all-just God whom they worship?

Psalm 88 is a good example if for no other reason than that it is as close to being a "hopeless" cry of grief as any of the biblical plaints. It is the lament of an individual Israelite whose life has been racked by sickness, exclusion and the temptation to despair. He stands on the threshold of Sheol, the pit of death, a place to which he feels he has already been consigned in terms of having been obliterated from Yahweh's memory:

> I am numbered with those who go
> down into the pit;
> I am a man without strength
> My couch is among the dead,
> like the slain who lie in the grave
> Whom you remember no longer
> and who are cut off from your care (vv. 5-6).[1]

Mortally sick over a long period of time, rejected by his friends, he is finally faced with the inevitable conclusion that even God has turned away from him:

> Upon me your wrath lies heavy,
> and with all your billows you overwhelm me.
> You have taken my friends away from me:
> you have made me an abomination to them;
> I am imprisoned and I cannot escape (vv. 8-9).

> Why, O Lord, do you reject me;
> why hide from me your face?

---

(1) Biblical citations are taken from **The New American Bible** except in those incidents where a direct translation or another text serve the interest of clarifying a point.

I am afflicted and in agony from my youth;
I am dazed with the burden of your dread.
Companion and neighbor you have taken away
from me;
my only friend is darkness
(vv. 15-16, 19).

The psalm does not end on an optimistic note; there is
no strong note of confidence as often characterizes the
lament. The psalmist has turned to Yahweh because he
must; there is nowhere else to go. The one thing that
could assuage his grief was some indication of Yahweh's
presence; in the absence of that, he can only conclude
that the Lord, too, has rejected him. It is only God's
wrath that he feels.

This deep, penetrating experience of evil on a personal
scale is often transposed to a new key in its being applied
to the nation as a whole. What the individual sufferer
experienced in his own life was a microcosm of Israel's
experience at the hands of foreign invaders. This is aptly
illustrated in the first chapter of Isaiah which critics
generally date from the end of the eighth century, the
time of Judah's King Hezekiah. The king had ill-advised-
ly allied himself with Egypt in the face of Assyrian
encroachment under Sennacherib. Assyria's retaliation
against Judah was disastrous for the country's cities and
villages, with little more than Jerusalem left in the wake
of the conquering hordes. This is reported not only in
the Old Testament but in the annals of Sennacherib as
well where Hezekiah is depicted as hemmed in "like a
bird in a cage." Isaiah's masterful presentation of Judah's
plight is not unlike that of a personal lament; it is the
picture of a slave, beaten and bruised, reeling with nau-
sea, at the hands of an angry master.

The whole head is sick,

the whole heart faint.
From the sole of the foot to the head
there is no sound spot:
Wound and welt and gaping gash
not drained or bandaged,
or eased with salve.
Your land before your eyes
strangers devour
(a waste, like Sodom overthrown) (Is 1:5b-7).

True, the prophet leaves no doubt as to why Judah is so afflicted. Sinful self-reliance and rebellion against its sole protector have evoked the divine wrath. Yet, it was the experience of misfortune on the personal level, so often inexplicable, which enabled the prophets to speak of national disaster with such vivid imagery.

As anguished as the cry of the Old Testament sufferer was, the experience of evil in itself was not the basic problem. This was part of the human condition and, as such, could be endured. The problem was basically theological and therein lay the agony. If it could have been posited that Israel's God was unjust, capricious or treacherous, this would have said little about God but would have gone a long way in explaining misfortune. The fact is that Israel was unwaveringly committed to the belief that Yahweh was just and fair. However bold the speech (for example in Job or Jeremiah's Confessions) there is no serious claim that Yahweh acts arbitrarily in his dealings with men. While much about him remained inexplicable and "wholly other," he was the God who, unlike men, remained beyond reproach.

Israel's neighbors to the east, related to her in so many ways, were not always of the same persuasion. They wrestled with iniquity no less than did Israel, but their conclusions admit of varying shades and hues. We find a Babylonian sage in the second millennium who, in view of the lot of the suffering just man, can only suggest that the moral order seems to be inverted:

> ... Oh that I only knew that these things are
> well pleasing to a god!
> What is good in one's sight is evil for a god.
> What is bad in one's own mind is good for his god.
> Who can understand the counsel of the gods
> in the midst of heaven?[2]

In "The Dialogue on Human Misery," sometimes called "The Babylonian Ecclesiastes," there is marked concern over the inequality evident in divine sanctions, although "the mind of the god is remote; his knowledge is difficult, men cannot understand it." But when the further question is raised as to why men act the way they do to incur the divine wrath, it is because the deities have made them so.

> The primeval king, the god Naru,
> creator of mankind,
> The glorious god Zulummaru,
> who nipped off their clay,
> The queen who formed them,
> the divine lady Mama,
> They bestowed upon humanity ingenious speech:
> Falsehood and untruth they conferred upon
> them forever.[3]

It was as unthinkable to Old Testament faith that Yahweh could be deceptive in his dealings with men as it was to suppose that he had given man a bent toward evil from the time of his creation. But the fact that

---

(2) Pritchard, J.—Ancient Near Eastern Texts, Princeton Univ. Press, 1955, p. 435. Henceforth referred to as ANET.

(3) ANET, p. 440.

Yahweh was just did not ameliorate the problem but only succeeded in aggravating it. Why then did the just suffer and the evil prosper? The answer proved elusive for centuries to the Israelite believer and, to a considerable extent, it remains so today. Yet, an answer was never sought at the expense of the God who had revealed himself as faithful and true. This alone says a great deal about Israelite faith.

The problem of suffering in the Old Testament cannot be detached from the more fundamental question of Hebrew anthropology and its corollary—survival after death. As contemporary biblical scholarship has been at pains to show, the Greek analysis of man as a body-soul composite is alien to Hebrew thought. In the second chapter of Genesis, it is the living God who activates the lifeless clay by his breath, "and man became a living being" (Gn 2:7). To say that Adam became an animated body serves to point up the fact that Hebrew **nephesh** is not an independent subsistent principle; it is very much identified with the body and its various parts which it inhabits. There is no thought here of the **nephesh** as the seat of intelligence (since the heart normally serves that function) or the other more "spiritual" operations proper to man; it is most visible in bodily functions and is frequently seen as manifesting itself in the breath (Gn 35:18; Jb 11:20; Jer 15:9) or the blood (Lv 17:14; Dt 12:23). In fact, man shares the same vital principle with other animate forms of creation[4]. Yet, in terms of man's singular place in the order of creation, mere animation says all too little. Once animated by the life principle, man operates in a way distinctive and superior to all other living creatures. In man, once vitalized, it is the "I" that emerges, and so **nephesh** in reference to man

---

(4) The **nephesh** is proper to all living creatures. Cf. Gn 1:21, 24; 9:10, 12, 15.

may often be translated as "person" or "self."

This is the understanding of man's composition which characterizes most of the Old Testament. It is basic to an understanding of the thorny questions raised by Job and Qoheleth. For Qoheleth, the "life breath" of man and beast are the same; the two enjoy the same lot since "one dies as well as the other." The conclusion is that "man has no advantage over the beast; both go to the same place" (Qoh 3:19-21). Life in man simply returns to God at death (12:7); it is fragile and wholly at God's disposition (Jb 34:14-15). Only in the last centuries before the Christian era will there be any breakthrough in terms of immortality. During the greater part of the first millennium, when most of the Old Testament was written, man's mortality was very much to the fore.

Death, then, became the great leveller; nothing was more terminal, more absolute. Whatever aspirations a man had were necessarily centered in his present existence. When a man died he lost that vital spirit which made him capable of thinking, feeling and responding to any possible stimulus. Life without the body was largely meaningless since every vital activity that man performed was identified with it. It was an obvious fact that death simply brought all of that activity to a halt.

Early Israelite tradition gave little attention to speculation about an afterlife, concentrating instead on the meaning of the present existence and avoiding the largely incongruous mythical fantasies of their pagan contemporaries on life after death. Sheol, or the pit of the dead, has no Christian counterpart. Most of what the Old Testament says about it is by way of negation, telling us more about what it is not than what it is. Qoheleth flatly asserts that in Sheol there will be "no work, nor reason, nor knowledge, nor wisdom." It is not even accurate to say that man "exists" in Sheol since he is without life, the use of the body, activity or passivity. What existence there is can be said to be akin to that of a shadow, transparent and nebulous. The most that Sheol allows us to say is that in some manner, vague and undefined, afterlife survival was admitted. Having said that, we have said little. The fact of the matter is that Sheol offers nothing to a solution of the problem of suffering or retribution. It is a place (or perhaps a state) from which even Yahweh was absent. There his praises are not sung (Ps 30:10; 88:12), nor is there any concern from his part (88:6). Yahweh is a God of the living, and it is with the living in the course of their mortal lives that he is concerned. Life for the Israelite meant not only the present world with its goods but the presence and experience of Yahweh as well. Thus, a life with health, family, flock and land—and even more importantly, a life lived in harmony with the Law of the Lord—was the greatest good that could be experienced.

It is hardly surprising, then, that the Israelite had such a revulsion toward death. This signified not only the terminus of his human existence but, even more significantly, in giving up his spirit his relationship with Yahweh was severed. Only the living man could worship and death effectively terminated that important avenue of access to the Lord which was central to Hebrew life.

> For among the dead no one remembers you;
> in the nether world who gives you thanks?
> (Ps 6:6).

The moral significance of death should not be underestimated. As Israelite thought developed, death was not considered as a natural inevitability. Man introduced it through his sin in Genesis; it is the supreme evil for which he is responsible and not God. When the psalmist prays to be delivered from death's throes, his reasons remain deeply religious; it is not simply because of an

inherent fear of death but because it represents a definitive separation from his God. It is this reference to what
might be termed spiritual or theological death that so
separates Israel from its Babylonian neighbors. The
nether world of Mesopotamia was no more inviting than
was Sheol; it was the "land of no return, the dark house
. . . the road from which there is no way back"[5], the
domain of darkness and dust. Man was created mortal
and "the world of the dead" is his inevitable destiny.
It is not a place of sanction for man's undoing; it is his
lot from the start. Israel found this inevitability of death
irreconcilable with her faith in a living and good God.
While she strained to give an answer to the problem in
a limited and highly figurative way, Israel stood unwaveringly by the belief that man was created for life,
a life that in some inscrutable way was originally destined to perdure. Through his sin, man had forfeited life
and before him lay only the gaping jowls of the under-
world from which there was no return.

The belief of Egypt in life after death contrasts sharply with what we find in Israel and Mesopotamia. The
variety of mortuary texts now available to us makes it
clear that the peaceful lot of the dead played a prominent
part in Egyptian thought. There can be no doubt that
death was seen as a transition, a passage to the necrop-
olis where all was peace and light. The monuments of
antiquity, for which Egypt is so well known—its pyra-
mids, sarcophagi, mummified forms—speak of continued
life. And scholars are prompt to point out that "continued
life" is, in fact, a more apt term than "future" or "afterlife." For, in the Elysian Field of Egypt, called the "Field
of Reeds," life differed from its earthly form only in as
much as it excluded its hardships and trials. Other than

---

(5) **ANET**, p. 107.

that, there was no significant difference, no bodily transformation, no essentially new state of being. The daily
course of events remained the same, with work and play
man's inalterable lot. Thus, the pyramid texts of the dead
monarch Unis presents him as still reigning, seated upon
his throne, scepter and wand in hand, giving orders as
he always had![6]. However, the Singer with the Harp
sees it as a land not to be belittled since it is characterized
by peace and serenity. In the land of eternity, "quarrel-
ing is its abomination, and there is no one who arrays
himself against his fellow. This land which has no opponent—"[7]

Why is such a belief in the hereafter nowhere found
in the Old Testament? In terms of its extensive historical
contact with Egypt, it can hardly be argued that Israel
was unaware of it. The answer would seem to lie in the
Egyptian concept of life after death, which would have
seemed grossly terrestrial and secular to Hebrew belief.
To see "eternal life" primarily as an extension of the
present existence was hardly a formidable breakthrough
to a people who saw the present life as circumscribed in
countless ways and whose greatest joy was found, not
simply in earthly pleasure, but in engagement in the will
and design of the living God. Eternity was Yahweh's
prerogative and, if man were to share in it, then it would
have to be on Yahweh's terms and in his company. It is
often suggested that some of the Psalms (for example,
49 and 73) reflect such a belief. The evidence is not in-
contestable but it is probable that the ultimate vindication of the just is seen in some form of positive survival.
These are rare instances and not representative of the
mainstream of Hebrew thought. Yet what seems to be

---

(6) **ANET**, p. 32.
(7) ibid., p. 33.

indicated is an ultimate deliverance which escapes the nether world and terrestrial limitation in some form of fuller life with God (Ps 16:10; 49:16; 73:23-24). Such minimal evidence, however, leaves little room for further speculation. Whatever is to be said for survival, Israel did not equate it with an earthbound prolongation of life. While the "good life" is not disdained, it is not elevated to a point where it became the fixed destiny of man. The belief in a God who was transcendent and spiritual precluded it.

There was, moreover, a theological meaning to death which is derived from the third chapter of Genesis. There, death becomes more than the simple terminus of human life; it is the penalty to be paid for rebellion. The bleakness of Sheol served as a reminder of man's sin, woven into human history from the start. Because of its connection with sin, it was inadmissible to think of death as a mere crossing of the River Styx or the passing through a door into another chamber where life, despite all its attractive features, was not really different than before.

It is quite true that the ultimate destiny of man in Israelite thought is very limited. There are no vast horizons; the idea of any personal life after death does not emerge with any force until the final centuries before Christ. There was, of course, the belief that one lived on in his posterity, and in his descendants a man attained some form of immortality. Beyond this, there was little more that could be said. The thought of death being so terminal is extremely difficult for the Christian to understand in view of the fact that so much of his religious and moral thinking is conditioned by his afterlife beliefs. This is not to say that it did not present difficulties for the Old Testament, and nowhere more significantly than in the area of human suffering. And yet it did not dim the Israelite's faith. The greater number of the Old Testament books, which stand among the noblest expressions of faith in world literature, were written in the belief that man's relationship with God is wholly measured in terms of this life. Yet, God was seen as a father, not a tyrant; his demands were to be taken no less seriously and man's response was to be no less committed. What much of the Old Testament fails to tell us about the life beyond, it succeeds in telling about the real meaning of faith.

Sin and Sanction

In the book of Numbers (ch. 32) it is related that the tribes of Reuben and Gad requested Moses to be permitted to settle in the region of Trans-Jordan prior to the invasion of Canaan by the Israelites. Moses is willing to permit this only on the condition that they first take part in the occupation of Canaan, at the successful completion of which they will be permitted to return to their land and families beyond the Jordan. In the course of the discussion, Moses says: "But if you do not (i.e., take part in the occupation), you will sin against Yahweh, and be sure your sin will find you out" (Nb 32:23). The verse aptly illustrates the intimate connection between sin and its consequences in Hebrew thought. The term for sin, hata', appears here in its verbal and substantive forms; in the former instance the emphasis falls on the sinful act itself and, in the latter, on the consequences of the action.

Man's moral transgression and its consequences can hardly be expressed in more concrete terms than in the Old Testament. Sin unleashes an evil force which, although it may wreak havoc in the lives of others, turns inexorably on its author like a boomerang. Critics have questioned whether or not sin had this quality of its own weight, quite apart from the consideration of divine sanction. It is quite likely that much of Near Eastern thought, which made no direct connection between man's moral conduct and a divine lawgiver, saw sufficient reason for the avoidance of misdemeanor solely on the basis of the act's inherent consequences. Within Israel, however, an essential nexus is established between law and Yahweh, its author. A man was observant because such was Yahweh's will, which will had also fixed the price to be paid for the disregard of divine mandate. Nonetheless, Israel was not unaffected by this strong interrelationship between sin and its self-contained consequences. As Gerhard von Rad states:

> Like a stone thrown into the water, every act initiates a movement for good or evil; a process gets underway which, especially in the case of crime, only comes to rest when retribution has overcome the perpetrator. But this retribution is not a new action which comes upon the person concerned from somewhere else; it is rather a last ripple of the act itself which attaches to its agent almost as something material.[8]

The word **hata'**, referred to above, appears most frequently as the term for sin. Its basic meaning is "to miss" or "to fall short" and is used in a variety of contexts. Thus Job is told that nothing in his household shall "be missing" (Jb 5:24) and Isaiah states that the man who "fails" of a hundred years shall be thought accursed (Is 65:20). Without any exclusively moral associations, the term is also used in the sense of missing the mark or falling short of a standard, e.g.,

> Where reflection is wanting, zeal is not good;
> he who goes too quickly **misses his way** (Pr 19:2).

---

(8) von Rad, G.; **Old Testament Theology**, Edinburgh, 1962, V. 1, p. 370.

Another term for sin which appears frequently is **pasha,** which carries the basic meaning "to rebel." Again, the word has no necessary moral connotation; it is used, for example, of Edom's revolt against Judah (2K 8:20). When the Sinai covenant established Israel's relationship with Yahweh along determined moral lines in terms of law observance, **hata** is the main word used to designate actions which fall short of the established norm. While the same idea obtains of failing to attain a standard, the norm now is one which has been given by God as part of a graciously bestowed "path to life" (cf. Dt 6:1ff.). A violation of the covenant terms is, by that very token, a violation of God's moral will.

Although much of later Judaism will come to view moral success or failure along dominantly juridical lines, as is seen in the climate of thought with which Jesus takes issue in the New Testament, such was not always the case. One cannot read the book of Deuteronomy without seeing sin as fundamentally an act of ingratitude, the violation of a love relationship. Yahweh was not seen as an imperial sovereign legislating for his subjects, but the partner in an alliance which he had freely established and of which Israel was totally unworthy. The Law was not seen as a consequence of this alliance, a way to show appreciation for having become God's own people. It was woven into the very texture of this binding relationship as the only way of life, or better, the way **to** life. The Law was an expression of God's benevolence, carrying within itself the motivating force for its observance.

To say that sin disrupted the relationship between man and Yahweh does not mean that this was always done consciously. It is difficult for us to understand how a man could sin inadvertently; yet this is simply a given in Old Testament thought. In the fourth chapter of Leviticus, for example, there is a list of sin offerings to be made by priests, princes, or the community for offenses committed unwittingly. But this represents no inconsistency when we recall the real, almost concrete character of sin. Once the act is performed, a disruptive force is released, with the consciousness of the perpetrator a secondary consideration. Ignorance may mean that a man is less culpable but it does not mean that the evil is less real. Even an unwitting agent disturbs the divinely-established order of things and is held to make amends with the hope that the evil of his action will not return to him. This partially explains why the sins of the father could be visited upon his sons. If the unleashed force failed to come to rest on one generation, it could well take its toll in the next.

An added consideration, often disconcerting to the modern reader, concerns the relationship between sin and uncleanness. A person could become unclean in various ways—through childbirth, skin diseases, menstruation—to mention a few. The condition made one unfit for cult and resulted in a state of separation from the community; purification rites were required before there could be full reintegration. While it would be incorrect to speak of uncleanness as a sinful state, it is strikingly similar to sin in its effect—alienation from God. Levitical penalties are imposed for both states. The sacrifice prescribed for the mother's purification after childbirth is referred to as a sin offering (Lv 12:6ff.). Such "excommunication" for situations which we would hardly term moral misdemeanor or offense against God is only understood when we realize that Israel embraced far more in the term "holiness" than we do. Man was related to God pre-eminently, but not exclusively, in the moral order. God was "other" (the basic meaning of "holiness" in Hebrew), and he belonged to a completely different order of things, an order of transcendence. Man in all his activity is summoned to approximate and reflect that "otherness"; in so doing, he not only observed the decalogue but avoided anything that might stain or contaminate his person. If the body person belonged to Yahweh, then the body person was to be kept integral; in a weakened, tainted or diseased state, it lacked a wholeness which rendered it unworthy of the Lord. To be part of cult and to be the member of a chosen people, integrity of the whole person, moral and physical, was essential.

Against this total background of sin Old Testament sanctions must be viewed. Since sin released a force which could be prevented from returning to the agent only by the staying hand of God, an intricate link is established between sin and punishment. Moreover, since sanction was seen as God's judgment upon man's sinful ways, it was demanded by divine justice. Sheol offered no hope of either positive or negative retribution. Death was the common end and the lot of men thereafter was the same for all. Therefore, if one's guilt is destined to catch up with him, it must happen within the context of his present existence. By the same token, if one lives virtuously, happiness in the present life, in terms of material prosperity, family, health and a long life, will be commensurate with his ethical posture.

Collective retribution, which also remains something of an anomaly to our highly individualistic ethical outlook, flows from all that we have said about the objective power of sin. It is moreover related to the quasi-physical unity which characterized societal groups in antiquity. The family, clan and tribe were the three core groups. The family included the husband, wife (or wives), unmarried children, married sons, their wives and children and servants of the household; the clan was constituted of several related families; the tribe, a group of clans believed to be descended from a single eponymous ancestor. In this way, the ties of blood, real or assumed, were established. In a very real sense, survival depended on group solidarity in ancient nomadic cultures. Concerted efforts did not have to be urged; they were facts of life. A lone traveller bore on his person the clan or tribal sign to forestall any ambush; any villain could recognize it as a certain sign of pledged reprisal. Within a tribe, all the members were permeated by a common spirit. No man was an island; his deeds affected the entire group. A tribal foray or a clan war meant total war, supported at least in spirit by all the non-combatants as well. By the same token, no one was exempt from the retaliatory action directed against such an effort. **Herem**, or total destruction, often left a village in ruins with no inhabitants, in its efforts to eradicate the total spirit of opposition. The evil had to be eliminated at its roots lest, like a dormant or hidden cancer, it re-emerge at some later date.

It is, then, not difficult to see how sin by the individual could take its toll on the group of which he was a member. It is connected with group solidarity and the infectious character of sin as a positive force. Thus, the Pharao and his household pay for his crime against Abraham (an unwitting transgression, at that!) (Gn 12:10-17), as do the families of Dathan and Abiram for the rebellion, of which the two were guilty (Nb 16:25-34). Depending on the gravity of the fault, retribution was envisioned as extending even to the third or fourth generation (Ex 20:5). The sure and effective way to forestall the retaliatory effect of an action on the community was to seek out the evildoer as quickly as possible with the hope of eradicating the evil at its source. In his pursuit of the Philistines, Saul receives no answer from the Lord when he inquires about the military strategy to be employed. He can only conclude that this is due to guilt in his ranks and, in casting the sacred lots, Jonathan emerges as the culprit, with Saul willing to put him to death lest the military fortunes of Israel be reversed (1S 14:36-44). Deuteronomy cites the case of homicide where the murderer remains unknown and prescribes a ceremony of propitiation with the community affirming its innocence in order to avert God's wrath (Dt 21:1-9). In the Yahwist tradition of the destruction of Sodom and Gomorra, there is a reverse application of the retribution principle (Gn 18:23-33). If evil is so communicable in its effects, why cannot the same be said of good? And so Abraham bargains with Yahweh to refrain from the destruction of the cities if there be found as few as ten just men. The Lord concurs, even though the minimal number will not be found.

In terms of the close relationship between sin and disaster, the lot of the nation was no different than that of the individual. Invasion, destruction, deportation—all were closely linked with Israel's wanton disregard of its covenant obligations. This was keenly felt in Israel where the life and destiny of the individual were indissolubly one with the destiny of the nation itself. This will be treated at greater length when we speak of the Deuteronomist; for the moment, it suffices to note the extent of the retribution principle in the moral thinking of Israel. The oracles against the nations, so frequent in the prophetic literature, follow the same line. Israel's traditional enemies — Moab, Edom, Ammon — have pitted themselves against Israel and so, by the same token, against Israel's God. Yahweh's justice could no more overlook an enemy's incursions against his people than he could disregard the failures of the people themselves. Moreover, sin was not restricted to Israel and, in its evolving consciousness of Yahweh's relationship to the moral posture of its neighbors, even though unbelieving, Israel gave geographical extension to its retribution principle. Thus, in Ezechiel, the trade-and-commerce minded Tyre is indicted for its haughty godlike attitude and the guilt involved in its sinful trade (Ez 28). The ruthless climax of Psalm 137 with its vengeful cry of destruction against daughter Babylon and its helpless children will never be understood against any other background except that which sees Yahweh's justice being meted out to Babylon in a manner commensurate with what Israel had suffered from its enemy. The scales had to be balanced if Yahweh, the vindicator of his people, was truly a saving god. Divine retribution had nowhere else to go except to a return in kind lest men say, "Where is your God?"

All of this is not to say that Israel's solution to the problem of suffering and evil was adequate; it obviously is not, as Job and Qoheleth will be at pains to point out. This is an affirmation which a more enlightened Christian reader can easily make. But the fact of the matter is that it is the solution with which Israel lived during most of its history, even during the Golden Age of its greatest literary achievement. Since it was a conclusion arrived at through experience, and therefore inductively, it ran into formidable difficulties when an attempt was made to give it broad application. When Hebrew sages were instructing young courtiers how to conduct their lives, the principle made good sense:

> The Lord permits not the just to hunger
> but the craving of the wicked he thwarts
> (Pr 10:3).
> He who walks honestly walks securely,
> but he whose ways are crooked will fare badly
> (Pr 10:9).

To say that virtue brings good fortune and misconduct spells disaster is a good principle of indoctrination and, in terms of a God who is just, it is good theology as well. The problem arises in starting with day-to-day experience and then making the principle fit. There was the rub. When one began his pedagogy with moral exhortation on the pursuit of virtue and the avoidance of vice, the truth could be well applied; when it came to explaining the presence of prosperity or misfortune, it was too simplistic to establish aprioristically the retribution principle. There were too many instances in which the facts argued against it. For a long period of time, Israel did not attempt to reconcile the differences; indeed, as we shall see, there were many moments in which, rather than leaving the principle broad, Old Testament thought became even more narrow and rigid in its application.

This failure to bring opposites into line, something which Western logic would find indefensible, is one of the intriguing features of biblical thought. While, for example, there is no question about Israel's ability to view poverty as a sign of Yahweh's judgment in numerous passages from the Wisdom literature and elsewhere, there develops concomitantly a theology of the **anawim,** the poor before God, which, according to Roland de Vaux, takes as its point of departure the materially impoverished in the community who had special claims on the community's concern and were to be the special beneficiaries of its largess (cf. Lv 19:9f; 23:22). The sense of dependence which was part of the lot of the poor came gradually to the fore as a necessary moral disposition for any man before God, regardless of his circumstances, a disposition which is integral to Jesus' teaching on the "poor in spirit." This example would seem to illustrate that Israel did make distinctions; some people were poor because they had alienated themselves from God while others were poor and could be considered the beloved of God. There were two sides of the coin, and neither can be said to have been neglected. But there was no attempt to integrate them into a synthesis. While neither admits of universal application, neither is devoid of truth. Old Testament man found that he could live with both of them. Yet, since much of the Old Testament is didactic in character and the Wisdom literature, with which we will be largely concerned, is dominantly instructive, it is the nexus between sin and evil that comes most to the fore. If nothing else, the example cited favors the position of those scholars who point out the difficulty of speaking of a single Old Testament theology, as if the approach to God and morality were unilinear and without deviation. There are a variety of theologies in the Old Testament (as well as the New), for the understanding of God in any age is multi-faceted. Theology is a very human endeavor, even when it is accompanied by inspired insight.

The Old Testament scholar, Walter Eichrodt, points up a number of positive features connected with Yahweh's judgment on human conduct which frequently distinguish Israelite thought from its neighboring cultures.[9] First, it is not whimsical; it has nothing of the satanic about it. While it often remains inexplicable, the scales are inevitably tipped in Yahweh's favor. He does not make of man a plaything nor is he accused of involving man in a guessing game. In fact, it was because God was seen as so inalterably just that the problem was so aggravating. In addition, wrath is never viewed as one of God's permanent attributes; rather, it is transient and operative in particular cases as a footnote to the covenant relationship. As the Psalmist says:

> His anger lasts but a moment;
> a lifetime, his good will.
> At nightfall, weeping enters in
> but with the dawn rejoicing (Ps 30:6).

Wrath is not seen as co-extensive with God's favor; it is commensurate with man's evil, but eventually runs its

---

(9) Eichrodt, W., **Old Testament Theology**, Phila. 1961, pp. 258ff.

course. Only the Lord's covenant love (hesed) and fidelity (emeth) remain forever.

> For I, the Lord, your God, am a jealous God,
> inflicting punishment for their fathers'
> wickedness on the children of those who hate
> me, down to the third and fourth generation,
> but bestowing mercy down to the thousandth
> generation, on the children of those who love
> me and keep my commandments (Ex 20:5).

Finally, the anger of Yahweh and its manifestations were part of his unsearchable "otherness." As part of God's nature, it was free of human assessment according to narrowly rationalistic categories of reward and punishment. As long as divine sanctions were explained along general lines, the situation was at least livable. It was only when what was seen as essentially mystery was subjected to an application that was overly narrow and rigid that the greater problem arose.

II.

ORIGINS, HISTORY AND JUDGMENT

To pinpoint the moment in Israel's history when evil in the world was identified with divine sanction on man's conduct would be a thankless task. The idea is woven into the texture of the entire biblical narrative. With our present realization that Old Testament "salvation history" is less a chronicle of events than a profound religious reflection upon them, we are more than ever aware that in examining a particular narrative we cannot say that the idea is primitive solely on the basis of its being found in an incident that occurred at an early date. Much of the material, for example, in the pre-history of the first three chapters of Genesis, is of very primitive legendary and mythical character. Nonetheless, it has gone through a process of theological refinement in oral and written form over such a long period of time in the history of Israel that it is in many respects a very advanced and sophisticated statement of religious belief. Consequently, when we speak of the origin of evil (Gn 2-3), there is no intention of affirming that Israel's (or man's) notion of religious sanctions began at that point.

For our present considerations, the book of Exodus serves as a fitting starting point. Therein, the high point of Israelite history is recorded in the exodus experience and covenant making at Mount Sinai. In Ex 19-24 we have the account of both the alliance itself and the terms of the alliance (chs. 20-23), which represents one of Israel's earliest law codes. After the people agree to abide by all that God has asked of them (24:7), the calf of gold incident (ch. 32) becomes a test case. This act of rebellion carries its own share of theological overlay and may be telling us as much about the syncretistic religious practices of the northern kingdom in the monarchical period several centuries later as it does about the people's waywardness in the desert. At least there is a striking resemblance between Aaron's forging the gold calf and the northern king Jeroboam's engagement in the same activity in 1 Kings 12:26-30. At any rate, in the text as it stands, the action of fashioning an image of the "God . . . who brought you out of the land of Egypt" (32:4) contravenes one of the basic provisions of the covenant terms. In the decalogue (Ex 20:4-5), it is contained as a corollary to the prohibition of idolatry in general; it receives an even more explicit expression in the legislation of Dt 4:15ff. At this point in the Exodus narrative, Yahweh's wrath flares up against his people (32:10); the evildoers are executed (32:27ff), and Yahweh refuses to accompany his people on their journey (33:3).

The God of Israel is, then, clearly seen in another dimension. He is not only the warrior God leading his people, or the mighty deliverer of the exodus; as a result of the covenant, he is seen as a God of love and concern to whom judgment and punishment are not foreign. He is a God of justice. In the succeeding chapters (33-34) of Exodus, a number of interesting insights on this whole question come to light.

In 33:18ff, Moses asks Yahweh to permit him to see his glory. Since it is axiomatic in Hebrew thought that no man can look upon the Lord and live, the narrator permits Moses only a glimpse of Yahweh "from the back" as the latter passes in front of the hollow of a rock where Moses is stationed. Chapter 34, which at least in part is the Yahwist's account of the covenant making in chapters 19-24, clarifies this highly anthropomorpic theophany.

> And Yahweh descended in the form of a cloud,
> and Moses stood with him there. He called on
> the name of Yahweh. Yahweh passed before
> him and proclaimed, 'Yahweh, Yahweh, a God
> of tenderness and compassion, slow to anger,
> rich in kindness and faithfulness; for thousands
> he maintains his kindness, forgives faults,
> transgressions, sin: yet he lets nothing go un-
> checked, punishing the father's fault in the sons
> and in the grandsons to the third and fourth
> generation.' And Moses bowed down to the
> ground at once and worshipped (Ex 34:5-8).

It does not seem to strain the evidence in seeing this passage as a commentary on Moses' "glimpse of God." What he comes to realize, after the calf of gold incident, is that the Lord's anger is no less real than his kindness and fidelity. Sin in its wanton disregard for the covenant terms will incur negative sanctions, just as covenant faithfulness evokes divine blessings. The calf of gold had been the first "test" of Yahweh after Sinai and it led to the clear conclusion that God would not be scorned. From this experience, according to the narration, Israel came to know more about its God, and it is this insight into God's nature that was adapted to the story of the "hindsight" view of the Lord which was granted to Moses. A patent connection is established between sin, suffering and sanction.

Beginnings

This same basic motif is found in the account of evil's origins in Genesis 2-3. As we have seen, one of the central theological problems in Israel was the reconciliation of evil as a reality with belief in a loving and constant God. The calf of gold incident arrives at an explanation in terms of God's sanction for covenant infidelity. But evil was not peculiar to Israel; it was shared by its neighbors as well. As Israel's vision expanded and Yahweh was related to all nations and not solely to his own people, parallel considerations also came to the fore. Sin had a cosmic dimension, as did its consequences—tragedy, misfortune, sickness, death. It remained for Israel to transpose its own experience to another key in explaining the universal presence of evil. This emerges as one of the central features of the early chapters of Genesis.

In the Yahwist account of man's creation and fall, the dominant concern is with God-man relationships, not with historical origins. For numerous reasons, contemporary exegesis now recognizes that Genesis is not whisking us back over thousands of millennia to the dawn of the first man's emergence to tell us how it all took place. In the main, the story of creation is a product of the first millennium B.C. in which important theological statements are made about Man (Adam), rather than a particular man. In fact, in Genesis 2-3, the Hebrew designation for the drama's human protagonist is simply "the man." It is not until the fourth chapter (Gn 4:25) that the appellation appears without the article as a proper name. In the Yahwist narrative, Adam is a collective personality, an individual representative of all mankind, and his conduct is not only representative of the earliest stages of man but, in a real sense, man throughout history, as the Israelite narrator saw him. Adam is not viewed simply as a "transmitter" of sin but as the archetype of man's sinfulness. That sin had its origins in the "twilight zone" of man's emergence and that subsequent stages in the history of man were affected by it is certainly present in the Genesis account. In fact, Genesis 1-11 is often called "the saga of sin" wherein the evolution of sin and its effects are graphically described. Yet, despite its affirmation of the primitive roots of sin, the Genesis didactic legend will never satisfy our curiosity about the concrete particulars of its origins.

What Genesis does affirm is that sin and its consequences are not of God's making, but man's. One of the dominant notes of the Priestly school's chapter 1 is that the created universe, all its inhabitants and man preeminently, come from the creator as good. The Yahwist in chapter 2 passes quickly over cosmic creation and rivets his attention on man. When, immediately after his creation, man is placed in the garden, a climate of friendship is established. In fact, the narrative is seemingly refracted through the Sinai experience with the covenant motif imprinted on the narrative. The divine initiative in covenant making is seen in the man's being taken and placed in the garden; this is followed by the precept regarding the tree and its subsequent violation. The naming of the animals underscores man's shared dominion over creation (not unrelated to the "image" of God, in ch. 1); in addition, placed as it is within the context of man's inhabiting the garden (2:18ff.), the episode is related to the theme of covenant friendship between man and God, who are partners in their presiding over the rest of creation. The idyllic picture of man's existence is marked by the absence of all those elements which the Yahwist realized scarred man's terrestrial life, such as sin, death, ignorance, arduous toil, and the pains of childbirth.

As we have already indicated, Genesis is not giving us a detailed description of man's first sin. This position has been abandoned in the light of our more recent understanding of the literary character of Genesis 2-3. In dealing with the pre-history of human existence, we are speaking of a moment in time about which even modern scientific inquiry has only the haziest notions. From a

strictly anthropological point of view, the origin of man
remains shrouded in considerable mystery, not to speak
of whatever religious sentiments might have been present in his most primitive stage of development. To the
plethora of questions about primitive man which are
raised by his twentieth-century counterpart, Genesis
does not supply the answer. What Genesis does affirm
is man's ultimate dependence on the Creator, his emergence as part of the inherent rectitude of creation, his
freedom of choice affording him fuller engagement in the
Source of his existence or its rejection, and the subsequent turning from God with its consequent disorder at
some point in the history of his development.

The manner of man's rejection of Yahweh is couched
in a literary expression marked by the interests and didactic concerns of the Yahwist author in the first millennium. In other words, "the sin" is presented along lines
which would be understood by the author's contemporaries, something common to their own ear, which would
serve well to remind them of their partnership in Man's
rebellion. The story's literary construction of man, woman and serpent, the search for broader knowledge, the
role of the couple's nakedness before and after the offense, as well as other features of the narrative, have
suggested to contemporary scholarship that we may be
dealing with a polemic against the fertility cults which
Canaanite culture had transmitted to the occupying
Israelites. In this religious expression, the deified forces
of nature, so essential to the well-being of an agrarian
people, were worshipped through sexual engagement
which, it was believed, could bring about a control over
the forces of life. In such cult, the serpent, as a symbol
of life, was an important ceremonial feature. Authentic
Yahwism found the whole expression abhorrent and
waged relentless war against any movement toward
Israelite co-existence with it or, even worse, any attemp-

ted synthesis with authentic Israelite belief. Shades of this polemic attitude may well be reflected in Genesis 2-3.

Another hypothesis would see the story in terms of man's grasp at moral autonomy. In eating of the "tree of the knowledge of good and evil," he expresses his desire to stand above good and evil rather than being its subject, a prerogative that belongs properly to the divine, not the human sphere. In this case, the serpent would be a symbol of wisdom and life. In either case, the story has a strong didactic tone. It is far more interested in underscoring the deep rupture between God and man which sin has effected from the beginning than in giving us historical data about sin's origin. Yet, in the total context of the book of Genesis, the chasm of sin is not unbridgeable. In the call of the patriarchs and the preparation for the espousal of a new people, the stage is set for a new era of the God-man relationship.

Directly related to our concerns is the nexus that is established between the sin of man and his subsequent lot. In the image of the struggle between the woman's offspring and the serpent, the stage is set for that unending conflict with evil which has beset humanity through the ages. While later tradition dwelt at length on the implied victory of man over the serpent, in underscoring the vulnerability of the latter's head, and hence the earliest biblical announcement of Christ's victory, there can be no doubt that the principal thrust of the text of Gn 3:15 is on the continuing and relentless state of enmity.

In the curses directed to the woman and the man in the Genesis text, physical hardships of life are presented as the consequences of sin. Examples are drawn from the pain and fatigue of human existence. The marital trials of the woman in childbirth, her sexual and domestic subjection to her husband and the arduous task of man in wrenching a livelihood from a difficult soil, contrast sharply with the earlier picture of equality between man

and woman and the idyllic peace of the garden where
the subordination of creation to man rendered even work
a pleasure. Now excluded from the "tree of life," man
finds his ultimate destiny in death as a somber climax to
the hardships of life. And this meant death in the Hebrew
categories already cited, the final and irrevocable sealing
off from the land of the living to cast one's lot with that
of the shades in Sheol. Sin had reaped its awesome toll;
to paraphrase Paul, its wages are anguish, toil and grief,
overshadowed by the awesome specter of death itself.

In relating sin and suffering, the author of Genesis has
drawn on the more obvious instances of human hardship.
He begins with man's lot as it is experienced in his own
time and relates it to the primordial sin. We may well
argue that all these factors are an intrinsic part of the
human condition, including physical death as man's natural destiny; it is a point difficult to contradict. But contemporary man's outlook was not that of the Yahwist
author and we do him no justice in making him say what
we understand. By reason of the sin, man, woman and
the world they inhabit have a different orientation—one
that is graphically described on the basis of human experience. The writhing snake, the pain of the expectant
mother, the sweat of arduous labor and the finality of
death served as concrete reminders of man's original and
continuing spirit of rebellion. Genesis does not speculate
about the ontological aspects of these realities; they are
cited for a moral and exhortatory purpose. The author
obviously believed that if there had been no sin, human
existence would have been different and notably more
felicitous.

But if human suffering and death itself are woven into
human existence, quite apart from sin, what then is the
message we can derive from Genesis? The answer should
be sought in the extent to which sin does color such realities. The basic lesson of the fall in Genesis is that man's

moral orientation has gone awry and, because of man's link with all of creation, his world, too, has been affected. This Genesis illustrates by listing some of the hardships of life which were familiar to all, moralizing in popular terms and not claiming scientific accuracy. Had fidelity to God rather than the selfishness of sin continued to characterize the activity of this free agent, much of the turmoil of man's existence would have been absent.

True, sin is essentially an internal reality, as a moral preferential choice for something other than God. Centuries ago, Tostatus, reflecting on the serpent's incongruous curse to become a crawling reptile, reasoned with wisdom that the "evil is more in the man than in the serpent." But the moral choice of sin, with its forsaking of God, casts a somber hue over the suffering of man, just as moral rectitude gives it a more positive and comprehensive meaning. It is one thing to endure hardship in faith, quite another to endure it in despair. Moreover, the concept of a life that does not end with the grave casts death in a completely different light. But it is a concept that the author of Genesis did not have. For him, death was terminal, destructive, the separation from all that was good. As such its cause must be sought in evil not in God. Genesis does not speak of it as the natural lot of man because its concern is with death as a spiritual reality. Human death is the definitive rupture in man's alienation from God. The author's belief that continued friendship with God would in some way have avoided such an end is, with necessary alterations, consonant with the clarification of later New Testament revelation. Neither Paul nor John, for example, in upholding eternal life as the Christian's destiny, exclude physical death as man's necessary lot. It is simply that Genesis was not in a position to make such distinctions. For Genesis, the "full life" involved the total living person and physical death was clearly its antithesis.

The centuries have seen a great deal of speculation on what life would have been like had there been no sin, and to a great extent it remains speculation. Genesis is much more concerned with what actually is than with what might have been, and the fact of sin was all too evident a reality in the culture of first millennium Israel in which the Yahwist wrote. It was also an accepted datum that the disrupted order of creation was not part of Yahweh's original design. All of creation had come from his hands as good. If the human lot is one of suffering and death, then it must be the consequence of man's undoing. Thus, the connection between sin and suffering is clearly established. The Yahwist has retrojected the experience of his own time onto the stage of man's beginning and finds there the initial rebellion which has left only human misery as its patrimony. Clearly, suffering is part of divine sanction, for Yahweh cannot disregard sin, but it is ultimately man himself who is responsible as the epic of sin grows to a crescendo in the subsequent narratives of Cain and Abel, the Flood and the Tower of Babel. Later offspring are presented as ratifying the perverse will of Adam as the evil force which has been unleashed continues to wreak its havoc. But the anguish of the human condition keeps apace, as sin reaps its harvest. This path of self-destruction, totally contrary to the divine design, cries out for a remedy, the remedy of God's saving power. Only with the call of Abraham is the downward trend halted, as the ground is laid for a new and different future.

The Deuteronomist

By the middle of the sixth century B.C., the Israelites had become a conquered and vanquished people. The northern kingdom of Israel had fallen to the Assyrians in 721 and Judah, to the Babylonians in 586. Bitter catastrophe had become the lot of that "precious possession" of the Lord, the child of destiny of the desert experience. The problems raised by defeat were far more than political or military; they were basically theological. The superior force of both Babylon and Assyria, which had succeeded in subjugating nations more formidable than Israel, could not satisfactorily explain the destruction of a people supported and championed by a God who was unique and all powerful. The prophets had often bargained for Yahweh's continued support by raising the question as to what the nations would say if Israel were to suffer defeat. Would they not inevitably ask: "Where is your God?" With the passing of time, the prophetic voice came to explain the nation's plight in terms of retribution for its sinfulness.

In the celebrated Vineyard Song, Isaiah speaks of the deserved lot of Judah:

> Now, inhabitants of Jerusalem and men of Judah, judge between me and my vineyard:
> What more was there to do for my vineyard
> that I had not done?
> Why, when I looked for the crop of grapes
> did it bring forth wild grapes?
> Now I will let you know
> what I mean to do to my vineyard:
> Take away its hedge, let it be trampled!
> Yes, I will make it a ruin (Is 5:3-5).

Or, again, the Lord complains in Jeremiah:

> I abandon my house,
> cast off my heritage;
> The beloved of my soul I deliver
> into the hands of her foes.
> My heritage has turned on me
> like a lion in the jungle;

Because she has roared against me,
I treat her as an enemy (Jr 12:7f).

The invaders are "rods of the Lord's wrath." So inevitable is the retribution to be visited upon Yahweh's people that efforts at defensive preparedness are futile; political alliances in the face of the threat will come to naught. Jeremiah's cry for capitulation before the enemy is seen as nothing short of treasonous.

The period of the Babylonian exile had a purifying effect. While never eliminating nationalist hopes, religious expectations became less circumscribed by geography and politics; personalism and universalism became more pronounced. The centrality of God's Word in Hebrew life, over against other considerations, comes more to the fore. It was also the moment for reflection on the past and the emergence of what can be termed a new theology of history in the work of the Deuteronomist.

The beginnings of the book of Deuteronomy are commonly linked with the discovery of a lost or concealed "Book of the Law" unearthed while the temple was undergoing repairs (2 K 22). This "miraculous" discovery is presented as the major cause of the far-reaching religious reform in Judah by King Josiah in 621 B.C., even though many modern critics wonder if it may not have been actually more supportive of Josiah's intentions than directly causative. The contents of the book probably originated in one of the cultic centers of the northern Kingdom and were brought south with the fall of Israel. This would represent the earliest edition of the book of Deuteronomy.

Since Deuteronomy came to grips with the "why" of war, devastation and exile, it served as a fruitful source of meditation during the major exile, offering at the same time a blueprint for the future. The early text grew into a new amplified edition, as it passed through priestly and legal hands, reaching its final form during the exile or the early post-exilic period. Its style is unmistakable, strongly exhortatory, basing obedience to its prescriptions on a heartfelt response to Yahweh's covenant love. In the catalogue of biblical books, we include Deuteronomy with the four books of the Torah that precede it, as the term "Pentateuch" implies. What modern scholarship has shown, however, is the literary and theological connection between Deuteronomy and the books that follow, i.e., the compendium of what we term the "historical" books—Joshua, Judges, the two books of Samuel and the two books of Kings. These books bear the Deuteronomist's imprint; they are an application to history of the principles enunciated in Deuteronomy itself. Literary and stylistic features common to Deuteronomy and the historical books are further evidence of a common hand.

Deuteronomy accents the prosperity and blessings that flow from fidelity to the Lord, as well as the tragic consequences that are inexorably linked with sin. "Do what is right and good in the sight of the Lord, that you may, according to his word, prosper, and may enter in and possess the good land which the Lord promised on oath to your fathers, thrusting all your enemies out of your way" (6:18f) . . . "But if you forget the Lord, your God, and follow other gods, serving and worshipping them, I forewarn you this day that you will perish utterly" (8:19). The weight of the Deuteronomist's effort is the vindication of this thesis as he traces the history of the chosen people from the period of the occupation of Canaan to the exile. Where there was covenant fidelity, or even a serious spirit of repentance, divine favor was not wanting; where there was wanton disregard of religious responsibility, in religious syncretism, social injustice, or rash political alliances, their lot was one of suffering.

In the book of Joshua there is a great deal of historical

condensation as the Israelites take possession of the land of Canaan with lightning speed. The length of the effort, and its accompanying difficulties, are of much less significance than the conviction that the land is a blessing, the clear evidence of Yahweh's fidelity to his promise. The land is invaded, its inhabitants dispersed, and the territory divided among the Israelite tribes. In the occupation the only major setback occurs at Ai (ch. 7). There the invaders suffer a reversal and defeat, not because of the enemy's superior strength, but because of the Israelites' violation of a ban against plundering the enemy booty. By confiscating precious goods that were to be dedicated to the Lord, they forfeited the subsequent victory against the force at Ai. Only when the principal culprit, Achan, is discovered and put to death, is there a reversal in the political situation. The problem called for a radical solution, the removal of the cancer at its source. We are faced again with evil's infectious character, in the elimination of the evildoer completely from the community, as well as that of solidarity in guilt in the extinction of Achan's family, livestock and goods. Only when these measures are taken is moral rectitude restored and victory against Ai assured.

The Deuteronomic leitmotif of sin and its consequences appears with particular clarity in the book of Judges. In recounting the celebrated deeds of these legendary figures of Israel's past, what we may call the "rhythm of evil," with its sequence of sin, punishment, repentance and deliverance, appears repeatedly. The Old Testament judges had one thing in common: they were all agents of liberation. According to Hebrew usage, the judge was one who achieved justice, and this in a twofold way. The judgment of which they were the executors brought vindication to the Israelites, only recently settled in Canaan, and, at the same time, it brought chastisement upon their foes. There is little that the judges have in common apart from their charismatic calling; their individual personalities, virtues and backgrounds present one of the Bible's most interesting studies in contrast. The basic literary pattern stamped on the narratives is not difficult to discern: some segment of early Israel sins, with divine punishment following in the form of an attack from some alien force. Made conscious of their wrongdoing, the Israelites "cry out to the Lord" and the divinely designated judge brings them victory.

In treating the question of evil, the Deuteronomist also sees adversity as a test of fidelity. The idea appears early in Judges. The very rapid occupation of Palestine depicted in Joshua is presented in more sober and realistic terms in Judges; it is all too evident that many segments of the earlier population remained long after Israelites had settled. In addition, there was the constant threat of foreign incursion from the Philistines, Phoenicians and others. In Judges, this continued presence is treated theologically. Foreigners were present to test the Israelites' endurance under stress (3:1-5). It is also stated that the presence of a threat would give the inexperienced military personnel necessary battle training but, more importantly, it is a test of moral stability. Surrounded by pagan forces, would Israel waver, become syncretistic, compromise its basic values? The stated fact of intermarriage (3:6) would indicate that the test was anything but an unqualified sucress.

This note of testing through adversity is a concrete illustration of an important teaching which goes back to Deuteronomy.

> Remember how for forty years now the Lord, your God, has directed all your journeying in the desert, so as to test you by affliction and find out whether or not it was your intention to keep his commandments. He therefore let you be

> afflicted with hunger, and then fed you with
> manna, a food unknown to you and your fathers,
> in order to show you that not by bread alone
> does man live, but by every word that comes
> forth from the mouth of the Lord. The clothing
> did not fall from you in tatters, nor did your
> feet swell these forty years. So you must realize
> that the Lord, your God, disciplines you even
> as a man disciplines his son (Dt 8:2-5).

The point is an interesting one. God instructs both
through blessings and through trial. Yahweh was as present to his people in their hunger as he was in their plenty.
The process of learning moved in two directions. In the
presence of affliction Yahweh "learned" whether or not
there was enough spiritual stamina for his people to per-
severe. Was this to be a people only faithful when it was
the recipient of benefits? In addition, the people could
learn through adversity, especially in deprivation, that
there are values that transcend material well-being, values which are the principal concern of religious experience. Basically, this is a consideration of the purifying
quality of suffering with which later biblical and post-
biblical writers will be greatly concerned. The Hebrew
verb **yasar** can mean both "to instruct" and "to chastise."
There is a lesson to be learned from adversity which
touches the core of man's relationship to God, and Hebrew culture with all its emphasis on the providential
aspects of the "good life," did not fail to recognize it.

Nonetheless, it is retribution for sin that is the constantly recurring theme in the litany of the kings of
Israel given in the books of Samuel and Kings. The reason
for the rejection of Saul as king comes to us in two ver-
sions: in one, he illicitly assumes the role of sacrificer
(1 S 13:8-14); in the second, he refused to obey the ban
in taking booty from the Amalekites (1 S 15). David, as

the faithful servant of Yahweh, brings the greatest blessings on his people, but his personal shortcomings are not excused. He is sharply admonished for his lust for Bathsheba and his wily machinations to effect the death of her husband, Uriah, in the parable of Nathan (2 S 12): sanctions for his sin will be forthcoming; there will be revolt within his own household in the person of his son, Absalom, and the child to be born of his illicit union will die. Notwithstanding his personal talents and political prominence, Solomon, too, suffers rejection for religious idolatry, syncretism and pandering to the interests of his foreign wives. He had contributed to Israel's international prominence and his talents were legendary but, in the Deuteronomist's eyes, his forsaking of the Lord outweighs all other considerations. The price must be paid. Upon his demise the kingdom will suffer an irreparable division (1 K 11).

After Solomon the picture becomes even more bleak as the ravages of sin continue in both north and south. In the main, the monotonous chronicling of monarchs finds them remembered for little else than that "they did evil in the sight of the Lord." That some of these reigns were distinctive by other standards is undeniable. The ninth century northern king, Omri, who established the court city of Samaria, was still remembered in the annals of Assyria a century after his death, wherein Israel is termed "the land of Omri." His idolatrous reign merits only six verses in the Deuteronomic history—little more than a passing mention (1 K 16:23-28). Just as the fateful drought, predicted by Elijah, does not abate until the evil is radically removed in the slaughter of the pagan prophets of Baal at the brook Kishon (1 K 17-18), Israel cannot expect the Lord's blessing and protection in the face of its wanton disregard of the terms of the Sinai covenant.

In a sense, history seems to move toward the destruction of both Israel and Judah with a certain inexorability. Hardened hearts were not softened. In the north, Assyria stood poised and ready to strike. That it was a massively superior force with imperialistic intent does not explain Israel's fall and exile for the Deuteronomist. The reason is simply stated: "This came about because the Israelites sinned against the Lord, their God, who had brought them up from the land of Egypt, from under the domination of Pharaoh, king of Egypt, and because they venerated other gods" (2 K 17:7). In the eighth-century south, Hezekiah's religious reform is well-intentioned but proves too limited and inadequate. In aligning himself with Egypt he makes what Isaiah calls "a covenant with death." As the Assyrian forces of Sennacherib move south, only Jerusalem is spared—and that due to the prayerful plea of Hezekiah (2 K 19). But the future offers little hope. There is a bright ray of hope for conversion in the much more effective reform undertaken by King Josiah, but even that dies at Megiddo with its champion. Sin has paved the way for Nebuchadenezzar and the Babylonian onslaught of 587 with the fall of the city, the temple and the monarch, and the deportation of a large part of the population.

The sixth-century picture is one of utter desolation. Great and lofty hopes had been trampled in the dust. A people, chosen and divinely commissioned by Yahweh himself, grovelled under gentile masters. As the Psalmist notes, there was little left to do by the rivers of Babylon except to sit and weep. The price of sin had been exacted in drastic terms.

But the period of the exile offered time for reflection and the possibility of a change of heart. The prophetic voice was eventually heard proclaiming a new return of the Lord and his people to their land. But the lesson of the past had to be a prelude to the future. In this, the Deuteronomist played a vital role. In reviewing past history he gave ample explanation for the evils to which Yahweh's people had become heir. For this sacred writer, and the school of thought for which he was the spokesman, the link between sin and suffering is secure. It is founded on the action of a just God, who will not be mocked, but also on that mysterious but undeniable bond which joins man's defiant choice and its frightening consequences.

Jeremiah

One of the most important and, in a sense, tragic figures of the last days of Judah was the prophet Jeremiah. The prophet of approaching disaster, he is unsurpassed in his penetrating analysis of Judah's moral state. If prophecy can be defined as three-fourths insight and one-fourth foresight, then Jeremiah is the prophet **par excellence**. While he echoes the traditional position on evil in terms of divine retribution, he also sees the impending disaster of Jerusalem's fall as a purifying experience. It is this idea of suffering as a form of divine discipline that comes to the fore in some of his most celebrated passages. He saw the destruction of Judah and Jerusalem as inevitable in view of the country's abandonment of Yahweh and the absence of any genuine conversion. Yet, he knew as well that the situation was not terminal and that, despite all, Yahweh's love was still constant. Hence, the present calamity was Yahweh's method of bringing his people back.

Certainly, the prophet had much to decry. The drift from fidelity, disregard of the Law, cultic profanation, mistreatment of the poor, sexual promiscuity, were open sores on the body of the once virgin Israel.

> Why should I pardon you these things?
> Your sons have forsaken me,
> they swear by gods that are not.

I fed them, but they committed adultery;
to the harlot's house they throng.
Lustful stallions they are,
each neighs after another's wife.
Shall I not punish them for these things?
says the Lord;
On a nation such as this shall I not take
vengeance? (5:7-9).

To the repeated summons to repent, there was no response.

When I raised up watchmen for them:
"Hearken to the sound of the trumpet!"
they said, "We will not hearken" (6:17).

The people continue to rely on their meaningless securities—their empty ritual, their temple, their sacrifices. The lament returns repeatedly: "They have forsaken Yahweh . . . They have forgotten the Lord . . . They have as many gods as they have cities." For Yahweh's part there is only one course of action left: to root up and tear down, to destroy and to demolish. He will bring evil in the form of the sword, desolation and deportation.

Yet, for Jeremiah it is a punishment that is not explained solely in terms of retribution; it is ultimately corrective and salvific. Out of the experience of evil and a leveled spirit will come a change of heart and a new beginning.

Cease your cries of mourning,
wipe the tears from your eyes.
The sorrow you have shown will have its
reward, says the Lord.
They shall return from the enemy's land.
There is hope for your future, says the Lord.
Your sons shall return to their own borders.

> I hear, I hear Ephraim pleading:
> You chastised me, and I am chastened.
> I was an untamed calf.
> If you allow me, I will return
> for you are the Lord, my God (31:16-18).

As has already been noted, there is an inherent force in the evil act which springs back upon the offender by its own weight. In Jeremiah it becomes a chastising force, not one which is simply retributive. Thus, in an important verse we read:

> Your own wickedness chastises you,
> your own infidelities reprove you (2:19).

It would not be unusual for Jeremiah to speak of Yahweh's chastising or reproving. What is striking is that the corrective force is attributed to the evil act itself. This is so because the bond between evil and its consequences is here seen in a different light; the destructive power emanating from evil is medicinal. It not only gives a man his merited punishment but can also bring him to his senses. Tragedy becomes curative.

Judah is purified by being stripped of its empty pursuits. Brought back to desert nakedness once again, God's people will be in a position to know their Lord. With no idols, no commerce, no temple or sacrifice, still bearing the wounds of their sinfulness, the people are brought face to face with their saving God. Yahweh looks upon his spouse in her destitution and says: "Now, **know** me once again."

Of particular significance in Jeremiah is his emphasis on what has become known as the "principle of personal responsibility," which influenced later thought on the problem of evil. It is evident in chapter 31, which speaks of the new covenant to be established between

Yahweh and his people, different from that which preceded in its strongly internal features (31:31-34). In speaking of the coming days, the prophet draws on a proverb which was evidently common coinage in his time in emphasizing the idea of collective guilt. He then promptly proceeds to reject it as a norm in his blueprint for the future.

> In those days they shall no longer say,
> "The fathers ate unripe grapes
> and the children's teeth are set on edge,"
> but through his own fault only shall anyone die:
> the teeth of him who eats the unripe grapes
> shall be set on edge (31:29f).

The change in emphasis is important even if its consequences are not to be exaggerated. Was it peculiar to Jeremiah or is he reflecting the thinking that had emerged out of the tragedy of his time? It is difficult to answer; certainly Ezekiel shares the same thought (Ezk 18:1f), but there are scholars who argue that he has drawn on Jeremiah.

It should be noted at once that Jeremiah, in his emphasis on the personal and the individual, never radically separates himself from the past. He still sees the new Israel in collective terms, the new covenant envisioned is one "with the house of Israel and the house of Judah" (31:31). He is not a champion of individual deliverance if by that is meant one which is separated from the lot of a redeemed people. His attitudes on retribution, with the exception of what has been treated earlier, are, in the main, traditional. There are no distinctions made on a personal basis in passages like the following:

> See, I will place before this people
> obstacles to bring them down.

Fathers and sons alike,
neighbors and friends shall perish (6:21).

In short, group solidarity is still an important factor in
Jeremiah and in more than one instance it is clear that
he has himself upheld the "sour grapes" principle which
he later disowns.

But the future is a different matter. In speaking of it
there is no denying that the prophet makes a notable contribution to the principle of individuality. Relationships
to God in the future will be rooted in a personal response
which will be judged on personal premises. The facile
cliche which attributes a man's unfortunate lot to the
wrongdoing of his progenitors will no longer hold sway.
Community solidarity and corporate personality, as important as they will continue to be, will no longer serve
as the escape hatch from individual accountability. In
retaining both the personal and the collective, Jeremiah
has juxtaposed rather than reconciled the two. It is not
unlikely that his concern for the individual was derived
from his own personal, anguished relationship to Yahweh
at a time when the nation's lot seemed destined to be one
of dissolution. The former covenant had failed and was
to pass with Judah's fall. The seed of a new concept of
retribution is already sown in the new covenant which
Jeremiah foretells. In a covenant of the heart, one that
touches the very core of man's relationship to God, com-
munal responsibility is necessarily somewhat eclipsed
as personalism comes to the fore. It is this strong inter-
nalization of covenant that enhances individual retribution.

No doubt Jeremiah understood from his own vantage
point that there is an interplay and not an irreconcil-
ability between the community and the individual.
Jeremiah's teaching was a necessary antidote to an over-

stated collectivism which could place praise and blame all too indiscriminately. It was not, however, a position which met overwhelming acceptance in the post-exilic period, fraught as the principle was with its own problems in its application to daily experience. Subsequent authors of the sacred books will continue to wrestle with the complex issue. While Jeremiah had carried the question forward in terms of the totality of revelation, he had at the same time presented a new set of obstacles for his contemporaries and spiritual heirs. Some of the most interesting chapters on the problem of evil and retribution were yet to be written.

III.

WISDOM: TRADITION AND OPPOSITION

My son, forget not my teaching,
keep in mind my commands;
For many days, and years of life
and peace, will they bring you (Pr 3:1f).

The words of Wisdom to her son reflect the traditional attitude on retribution which continues to hold sway in much of the post-exilic Wisdom literature. Fidelity to Yahweh's teaching will bring blessing, while its disregard will bring misfortune. Often called the Deuteronomist theory, it raised as many questions in the practical order as it proposed to solve, but there is no question about the fact that it was the theological position in possession. It was perhaps in the light of Jeremiah's emphasis on individual retribution that the principle became even more precise with a relationship between action and sanction of an almost quid-pro-quo exactitude.

It is difficult to date much of the Wisdom literature of the Old Testament. Its beginnings are to be found in the **mashal,** the brief proverb or maxim, which served as a guide to correct living. The person who lived in accord with such directives was wise, in a very concrete and practical sense of the word. Many authors find the original historical setting of this type of literature in royal scribal circles of the king's court in the early days of the Hebrew monarchy. Many of the sayings found, for example, in the book of Proverbs, would derive from this period. However, the literature evolved with the concept of wisdom itself. As Yahweh was seen to be the source of all true wisdom, there is considerable speculation on this as one of his attributes. As questions arose as to the meaning of life, much of it precipitated by the application of the **mashal** to the complexities of daily living, the genre of wisdom was expanded to include lengthier disquisitions as reflected, for example, in the books of Job and Qoheleth. Hence, attempts at dating the books depend almost wholly on the internal evidence of this type of evolution, with some material representing an early stage of development and some, a more advanced. Specific historical references in the books are relatively rare.

The book of Proverbs represents both the earlier and later stages of development. The two Solomonic sections (chs. 10:1-22:16; 25:1-29:27) could well date from the time of Solomon; yet the book as a whole is a product of scribal activity after the exile. Hence, while it would be incorrect to state that its teaching on retribution is a post-exilic development, there is no doubt that the traditional teaching on the subject was both accepted and upheld by the author. Proverbs can then be treated as a conservative source for the problem of retribution. It neither makes important breakthroughs nor questions the achieved position.

In Proverbs, if one desires riches and honor, abundant crops, family, good health, a long life, or the "good life" in any sense, it is to be achieved through virtuous living, which is expressed as the pursuit of Wisdom. She comes laden with her riches:

> Long life is in her right hand,
> in her left are riches and honor (3:16).

If the Lord is honored with the goods received,

> Then will your barns be filled with grain,
> with new wine your vats will overflow (3:10).

There is no doubt that a morality which looks for sanctions in the here and now can and does lead to a type of pragmatism which seems excessively mundane. Does not the Old Testament itself offer nobler motivation for doing good and avoiding evil than the temporal consequences of one's choice? There is a proverbial truth in the assertion that "he who gives to the poor suffers no want, but he who ignores them gets many a curse" (28: 37), but it is hard to propose as an ideal, especially in the light of what the Old Testament itself commends in terms of the "poor of Yahweh." There are biblical reasons for avoiding the company of prostitutes, quite apart from the loss of money involved (29:3), just as there are reasons for avoiding idleness, other than the pangs of hunger one is destined to feel. Yet, wisdom morality is distinctive and must be accepted on its own terms. The formulation of the earliest maxims was rooted in experience, not in moral abstracts. The sages offered highly practical advice to one who tried to steer a safe course through the stormy waters of daily life. Both the action counselled and its consequences, for good or evil, were the products of experience and were broad enough in their application to be admissible. Looking as they do at only one aspect of a situation, proverbs have a limited value. A counter statement, which "looks at the other side of the coin," can make this all too evident.

The limited scope of the wisdom sayings is both its strength and its weakness. Rooted so strongly in experience, their sense can readily be grasped as well as the validity of the point they are making. Yet, in all too many instances, it is experience itself that belies them. This is particularly true in the matter of retribution. It it too simplistic to assert that the "good life" comes from virtue and that human ills come from vice. This is especially true if one is poor, rejected or suffering, but the maxim was probably questioned as well by many a comfortable landowner, at least in his more sober moments. It is this "other side of the coin" of many of the proverbs that cut deeply into the Hebrew conscience and led to the subsequent questioning of the very truth they assert.

The strongly traditional author of Proverbs does allow, however, for the disciplinary and probative aspects of adversity. He would not argue that retribution is its only **raison d'etre**. He takes up an idea which, if not new, is at least helpfully qualifying.

The discipline of the Lord, my son, disdain not: spurn not his reproof; For whom the Lord loves he reproves and he chastises the son he favors (3:11f).

Thus, the Lord's favor and love can be at work in adversity; punishment is not a sign of irrevocable alienation. If it serves to bring a man to his senses and to a conversion of life it has served a worthy purpose and, distasteful as it may be, it can bring about a realization of God's goodness and his desire to save. In addition, hardship can also have a testing value as in the case of the trials of the desert experience. How else is Yahweh to know the genuine fidelity of his people?

The crucible for silver, and the furnace for gold, but the tester of hearts is the Lord (17:3).

This, too, is a truth rooted in experience and history has repeatedly given it support. The strength of moral conviction emerges when it is put to the test. It is never difficult to conform when it is the accepted thing to do or when the cost is minimal. But when faith is immersed in pain it either vanishes or is purified and strengthened. Proverbs does little to expand on these two important notions of discipline and testing; the emphasis on suffering as sanction comes much more to the fore. But the fact that the author has included them is itself a hint that he realized there was no single or simple answer to such a complex question. Yet the overarching principle remains the same. The fullness of life, always identified with the present world, lies in the observance of justice while death, in Sheol's realm, the antithesis of everything that life connotes, is the inevitable fruit of wickedness (11:7; 12:28; 15:24).

This same line of reasoning is found in the work of Jesus, son of Sirach, writing in the early decades of the second century B.C. The book of Sirach (frequently referred to by its Greek and Latin title, "Ecclesiasticus") was written in Hebrew by a Jerusalem sage and some fifty years later translated into Greek by his grandson. It was this Greek version that enjoyed extensive popularity in early Christianity and, until the more recent discovery of a large part of the original Hebrew text, was the source of subsequent translations. Sirach, a devout Jew, was steeped in the traditions of his people, deeply attached to all of Israel's sacred institutions. One of the last contributors to the wisdom tradition, he is heir to the patrimony of his scribal forebears.

Of particular interest, at this relatively late date of composition, is Sirach's strong adherence to the traditional teaching on retribution, notwithstanding the fact that the doctrine had been subjected to serious scrutiny in the meantime. In this regard, there is little difference between Proverbs and Sirach.

Do no evil, and evil will not overtake you;

> avoid wickedness, and it will turn aside
> from you.
> Sow not in the furrows of injustice,
> lest you harvest it sevenfold (7:1f).

Retribution is strongly individualized; evil will take its toll before the grave is reached.

> Rejoice not at a proud man's success;
> remember he will not reach death unpunished
> (9:12).

Death is so final that the present life calls not only for proper conduct but the wisdom of a certain enlightened self-interest.

> Give, take and treat yourself well,
> for in the nether world there are no joys to seek
> (14:16).

Even grief over the death of a friend should not be carried to excess lest one's health be impaired (38:18-21). Life is the greatest good, its only surrogate being its prolongation in the memory of a good name (41:11-13) or the family line (30:2-6). Like Proverbs, Sirach admits that the trials of life can deepen faith and lead to a stronger adherence to the Lord (2:1-6). Even death can be seen in a positive light when it represents the end of human woes (40:2). Yet it is this very finality of death that so confines Sirach, as it did his predecessors, when confronted with the aching problem of evil. As a theologian he must uphold the justice of Yahweh at all costs. Therefore, as difficult as application may be in the concrete, he faithfully transmits the mindset of the past.

This traditional position, so strongly emphasized by the Deuteronomist and sharpened even more in Jeremiah and Ezekiel, has to this point gone largely unchallenged.

But when it comes to the question of evil, not to speak of other areas, the Old Testament is not a theological monolith. Other forces were at work in post-exilic Judaism; it was a period of religious ferment in which new answers were being sought to many of the old questions. And certainly the contradictions between theory and reality, with which the conservative position on retribution failed to come to grips, provided fertile terrain for further scrutiny. The book of Job is probably the most celebrated example of this questioning of "first principles."

The Book of Job

Job is wisdom in the broad sense of the term; it is not a collection of maxims. Neither in style nor content is it the same; in fact, its whole thrust is at odds with the brief "ready answer" approach. It is wisdom inasmuch as it is an attempt to explain one of the enigmas of life, with practical experience as its starting point, and this evolving into a lengthy theological inquiry on the question of adversity, and its role in the relations between God and man. This it does in a poetic and dramatic fashion.

As a literary work Job is a composite. The prologue (1:1-2:13) and epilogue (42:7-17) represent an originally single story about the suffering just man which, judging from its Mesopotamian and other Near Eastern parallels, could well date from the early second millennium, at least in its earliest non-Yahwistic form. Dates on the composition of the book as a whole, however, remain conjectural with estimates spanning a thousand-year period. Both on the basis of language and theological content, we can safely opt with many modern authors for a date within the first two centuries after the exile in Babylon. There is no doubt that the burning question of individual retribution, which the book addresses, was at the center of post-exilic speculation.

The story as presented in the prologue and epilogue is familiar enough. Yahweh permits Satan, the tester and a member of the heavenly court, to subject the faithful Job to a series of calamities in the interest of testing his fidelity. Despite the loss of family and property and the torment of disease, Job's constancy never wavers. He is amply rewarded in kind with the subsequent restoration of family and fortune. It is a classic illustration of the traditional teaching on retribution. The suffering in this case is not for personal wrongdoing; rather it serves as a test. When the hero has sufficiently proved himself, his virtue is more than adequately rewarded.

This simple tale lent itself ideally to an inquiry into the whole question of retribution. Its use of dramatic irony permits the reader to know the testing purpose behind the suffering of Job while the protagonist of the story remains ignorant. Therefore, a later author took the early tale and built within it the lengthy discussions between Job and his three friends, as well as the speeches of Elihu and Yahweh, around one central theme: Why does Job, the just man, suffer?

Does Job come up with a new solution to the age-old problem? If we are thinking in terms of significant breakthroughs, the question would have to be answered in the negative. Job never abandons the traditional view espoused by his friends even though he questions it and cannot accept its applicability in his own case. If there were any other solution available, the treatise could have taken quite a different direction. But if, as we believe, the Deuteronomic position has come down to the author of Job, refracted through Jeremiah's strict equation of individual retribution, then the time had come for that position itself to be put to the test for the simple reason that it too often contradicted man's experience. Job refuses to render lip service to a position which, even if it does give God his due, does rank injustice to man himself. Thus the author courageously raises an important question and, while not gifted with the ultimate solution, gives us stunning and timeless insight into this age-old dilemma.

Since the reader is advised at the book's beginning that Job is being tested, one wonders why such a plausible explanation is not given ample treatment in the discourses between Job and his friends. The fact is that Job's test serves, at best, as a backdrop to the story in upholding Yahweh's moral autonomy and avoiding any idea of divine caprice. For the purposes of the book's author, it is essential that Job suffer without reason, making inapplicable the traditional tenets on retribution. Job's own experience offers no satisfactory explanation for the deluge of woes to which he has been subjected. He is guilty of no wrongdoing; the arguments of his friend have no cogency. Of the first, Eliphaz, he asks for evidence of his moral failure.

> Teach me, and I will be silent;
> prove to me wherein I have erred.
> How agreeable are honest words;
> yet how unconvincing is your argument!

> Think it over; let there be no injustice.
> Think it over; I still am right.
> Is there insincerity on my tongue,
> or cannot my taste discern falsehood?
> (6:24-25; 29-30).

At first Job fears to contend with Yahweh: "For he is not a man like myself, that I should answer him, that we should come together in judgment." (9:32). He is quite willing to settle "out of court," if only the heavy hand of the Lord be lifted:

> Are not the days of my life few?
> Let me alone, that I may recover a little
> Before I go whence I shall not return,
> to the land of darkness and of gloom,
> The black, disordered land
> where darkness is the only light (10:20-22).

The analyses of Job's friends only augment his agony. They are detached and self-righteous, mouthing their skillfully drawn conclusions which offer Job anything but solace. Eliphaz begins with the principle that no one suffers unjustly and evil actions beget sad consequences:

> Reflect now, what innocent person perishes?
> Since when are the upright destroyed?
> As I see it, those who plow for mischief
> and sow trouble, reap the same.
> By the breath of God they perish
> and by the blast of his wrath they are consumed
> (4:7-9).

Deductive reasoning convinces him that God finds fault with every man (4:17ff.) and leads him ultimately to catalogue Job's sins (22:5-11), rash assertions which Job repeatedly denies. But, he states, Job is to take heart, for suffering has its purifying effect which will ultimately make him a better man.

> Happy is the man whom God reproves!
> the Almighty's chastening do not reject.
> For he wounds, but he binds up;
> he smites, but his hands give healing (5:17f.).

Clearly on Yahweh's side, Bildad, the second friend, unfalteringly echoes the justice of divine treatment. If it is a contest between the Lord and Job there is no doubt as to where one must cast his lot; the only course left open to the hapless sufferer is to save his breath and turn to the Lord in prayerful supplication, even if the picture is badly blurred (8:1-7). The third friend, Zophar, feels that he has little new to add to his comrades' reproaches but it is noteworthy that he is at no loss for words to prove the point. After the disquisitions of the three antagonists, it is sheer irony to be faced with Zophar's caustic references to Job's long-windedness and babblings (11:1f.).

In the face of all this Job can only assert that this lengthy theologizing finds no echo in his own life. The traditional position on retribution is simply not watertight; his own life is proof of it. In some of the strongest expressions to be found in the Old Testament, he reaches the point, undoubtedly in desperation, wherein he can see his treatment by Yahweh as unjust.

Be it indeed that I am at fault
and that my fault remains with me,
Even so, if you would vaunt yourselves against
me and cast up to me my reproach,
Know then that God has dealt unfairly with me,
and compassed me round with his net.
If I cry out "Injustice!" I am not heard.
I cry for help but there is no redress (19:4-6).

With all possibilities of an adequate explanation exhausted, Job finally makes an impassioned plea of innocence which goes beyond avoiding violations of the Law to an active pursuit of virtue (chs. 29-31). There is no rhyme or reason to what he has been forced to endure—unless the Almighty should choose to step forth and give answer! On that note "the words of Job are ended."

But the contest is not yet concluded. Job is not even entitled to the final word. Another "theological" friend is waiting in the wings and promptly takes center stage before the major climax. The Elihu speeches (chs. 32-37), wordy and adding little to the argument of the three friends, are awkwardly situated after Job's final plea and prior to Yahweh's dramatic intervention. Many authors see them as a later insert, dulling the dramatic impact of the Job-Yahweh confrontation. Elihu's is a lengthy monologue, reiterating much that has already been said. He admits that Job has not been convicted, but the same can be said of the Lord. He reminds his hearers that suffering can be disciplinary, instructive and purifying (33:14-33), and hence a blessing in disguise. He prepares the way for Yahweh's appearance in upholding the inscrutable ways of his transcendence. Yet, despite all the fanfare accompanying Elihu's unexpected appearance in the narrative, he proves to be quite anticlimactic. When he makes his exit, the basic problem is still very much to the fore.

It is in the book's final moments that Yahweh speaks to Job out of the angry storm in two major speeches which in their soaring lyric quality are justifiably recognized as one of the Bible's literary highpoints. Basically, the poetry of chapters 38 through 41 takes the form of interrogation in which the Lord confronts his opponent. In keeping with his complete "otherness," Yahweh does the questioning; he himself is not questioned. He will not be involved in a verbal duel with the mortal Job. Yet he does respond. His answer moves immediately away from the particulars of the preceding debate and rises to his overarching attributes of wisdom and power. In the face of that wisdom, which creates and orders the universe from its heights to its depths, the Lord can ask: "Who is this that obscures divine plans with words of ignorance?" (38:2). Before the might that can treat the frightening mythological sea monsters like domesticated pets, "would you refuse to acknowledge my right?" (40:8). The argument has shifted to a new level in a reaffirmation of Yahweh's supremacy and transcendence. Man's limited intelligence cannot possibly plumb the depths of the divine. By the same token, it can be concluded that this same wisdom and power are capable of solving enigmas with which man can only grapple. Yet the issue, as Job presented it, is completely ignored; the why of his suffering remains unexplained. There is no denial of his protestations of innocence, so in one sense he seems to have been vindicated. But neither is the traditional argument discarded. The answer lies in mystery before which man's response can be only faith. We have returned to the prologue's point of departure: "The Lord gave and the Lord has taken away; blessed be the name of the Lord" (1:21).

Job walks a narrow path between two abysses. On the one side, the author avoids the facile but unsatisfactory solution of attributing evil's presence in the world solely to the wrongdoing of its victim. On the other, notwithstanding his protagonist's impassioned outburst of ill treatment (19:4-6), the author of Job never seriously entertains the possibility of divine injustice. This is a far cry from the Sumerian myth's attribution of the origins of physical deformities to drunken gods at play or the Babylonian sage's tracing of moral and physical evil to divine creation itself. Such a position would be inadmissible for Job's author; the divine will is inscrutable but it is not unjust. Yet Job honestly confronts the Deuteronomic theory and, while proposing no alternative theory, leaves the traditional position substantially weakened. Had there been even a glimmer of eternal sanctions beyond the grave, the protagonist's anguish would have been considerably alleviated and the whole thrust of the book, different. Despite suggestions to the contrary[1], the whole tenor of the book reflects a period wherein the entire question of retribution was contained within the limits imposed by human mortality.

It would be a grave error to conclude that in the light of later revelation such limitations make Job's message irrelevant. As we shall see, human suffering takes on important new dimensions in the light of the cross; yet, even with the significant insights offered by the New Testament, the mystery remains, a mystery which demands a living faith. Indeed, one wonders if there is a crucible in which faith is more strongly tested and fortified than in that of suffering. The echo of Job's question is found in the life of Jesus himself as well as in the lives of the sainted figures of Christian history. There is a lesson in Job which many of us have yet to learn. Faith is not a traditional convention; it cannot be reduced to what Bonhoeffer appropriately called "cheap grace." Faith is brought to life through struggle and spiritual agony. It cannot escape the inevitable "Why?". The anguish of human existence is its fertile terrain, offering the opportunity to walk with the Lord no more or to turn to him with even greater abandon. Job never received an adequate answer to his question but he ultimately made a surrender in faith. There are moments when we can do no more. At the risk of doing injustice to the poetic greatness of the Lord's response to the troubled Job, the message remains powerfully succinct in its conclusion: "Trust me!".

_____

(1) The famous text of Jb 19:25-27 cannot be said to alter this view. Its poor state of preservation in the Hebrew presents major obstacles; at best it presents an urgent plea for Job's eventual vindication but there is no adequate evidence that this hope reaches to the other side of the grave.

The Book of Qoheleth

Within the body of the Wisdom literature of the Old Testament, no book registers more dissatisfaction with the traditional theory of retribution than Qoheleth. In many ways it is a difficult book—even its title is not clear. More commonly known by its Greek and Latin name, "Ecclesiastes," the Hebrew Qoheleth refers to someone related to an assembly or congregation, thus giving rise to Luther's "Preacher" or, with others, "The Teacher." Whatever his function, he assumes the role of Solomon, Israel's archetype of wisdom. The attribution is wholly literary, however, since the composition, on the basis of its content as well as its use of Aramaisms and Persian expressions, is seen as post-exilic, probably dating from the third or fourth century.

Qoheleth takes many of the tenets of traditional wisdom to task; he examines them and finds them wanting. Forms of speculation on the meaning and purpose of life are doomed to failure, an empty and fruitless pursuit. It is the supreme vanity, in an expression used repeatedly in the book, a vapor or a wisp of smoke, indicating the transparent and vanishing quality of everything mortal, whether it be man's work, his pleasure or his philosophizing. The fact is that we find ourselves caught up in a fixed and predetermined order of things which only the fool would attempt to alter. Man is inserted into this bigger-than-life. drama, plays his part and makes his exit, as unknown after his departure as he was before his entrance (1:2-11). The indefatigable worker or the future planner waste their time in thinking they can extricate themselves from this web of predetermination.

So my feelings turned to despair of all the fruits of my labor under the sun. For here is a man who has labored with wisdom and knowledge and skill, and to another, who has not labored

over it, he must leave his property. This also
is vanity and a great misfortune. For what profit
comes to a man from all the toil and anxiety
of heart with which he has labored under the
sun? All his days, sorrow and grief are his
occupation; even at night his mind is not at
rest. This also is vanity (2:20-23).

Then there are the famous "times": a time to be born,
and a time to die, a time to love, and a time to hate, a time
of war, and a time of peace (3:1-8). The litany is not
intended to move man to action or to bring a halt to the
"times" which oppress. Quite the opposite. Such unending cycles in their tiresome monotony are a reminder to
the truly "wise" man that there is nothing he can do to
change a thing. One cannot "pilot his own ship" or master
his own destiny. He must simply resign himself to the
inevitable and the unchangeable. In fact, the whole life
process escapes any attempt to understand it or to see
the total process. As soon as one makes an affirmation,
daily life is sure to contradict it. Yet, with it all, Qoheleth
remains a man of faith—faith in God's creative and
providential will. But as to the "great design," he asserts
that man has been left in the dark. That is the Lord's
realm and he remains apart. Attempts to explain the
divine plan are an exercise in futility and, as Qoheleth
sees it, the "wisdom" of the traditionalist sages supports
the thesis.

Can it be said that virtue receives its reward and vice
its punishment within this fixed framework? Quite the
contrary, says Qoheleth.

This is a vanity which occurs on earth: there
are just men treated as though they had done
evil and wicked men treated as though they
had done justly. This, too, I say is vanity (8:14).

Indeed, it is the sinner who multiplies his evil and continues to fare well. In the eyes of men he is often a man of prestige receiving the accolades of others (8:10f.). The picture is so contradictory and the final lot of both good and bad so identical that from a human point of view the line between virtue and vice seems to have blurred.

> All this I have kept in mind and recognized;
> the just, the wise, and their deeds are in the hand
> of God. Love from hatred man cannot tell;
> both appear equally vain, in that there is the
> same lot for all, for the just and the wicked, for
> the good and the bad, for the clean and the
> unclean, for him who offers sacrifice and him
> who does not. As it is for the good man, so it is
> for the sinner; as it is for him who swears
> rashly, so it is for him who fears an oath. Among
> all the things that happen under the sun, this
> is the worst, that things turn out the same for
> all. Hence the minds of men are filled with evil,
> and madness is in their hearts during life; and
> afterward they go to the dead (9:1-3).

How then can it be said that evil eventually convicts a person, when experience gives so much evidence to the contrary? So skeptical is Qoheleth that he sees such a response as nothing more than a palliative which he repeatedly rejects. The fact that he does recognize sanctions at one point may come as a surprise:

> Though indeed I know that it shall be well with
> those who fear God, for their reverence toward
> him; and that it shall not be well with the
> wicked man, and he shall not prolong his shad-
> owy days, for his lack of reverence toward
> God (8:12f.).

Critics have suggested that this may be the addition of a later (corrective) hand or a satirical juxtaposition of different ideas in the same context in a sort of **reductio ad absurdum**. Such does not seem to be the case. The affirmation is made along very general lines and the author realizes that it must in some way, however indiscernible, have its element of truth. To argue the opposite categorically would be to make a mockery of God's justice. But he simply states it and makes no attempt to explain. In general lines it can be upheld since Yahweh cannot see evil as good. But how it is worked out in the concrete is beyond man's ability to grasp and Qoheleth is not about to add his name to the long list of those who have given ample proof of this incapacity.

Moreover, the future holds no prospects for a solution. What can be said for Sheol where there will be "no work, nor reason, nor knowledge, nor wisdom" (9:10) and, quite logically, no recompense? The present life is all one has so "better a live dog than a dead lion" (9:4). Without the hope of a meaningful afterlife Qoheleth has carried the question of retribution to its inevitable conclusion. The author has been accused of pessimism, cynicism and audacity, but there is no escaping his fearless honesty. He goes beyond Job in rejecting earlier explanations but lacks the latter's spirited contestation. He does not pit himself against Yahweh nor does he say there is no answer. The whole thesis of the book points up the inalterable character of a fixed divine order and the question of retribution is a part of that thesis. In the matter of evil, as in so many other things, man's understanding is extremely limited. Unless one is willing to accept that fact, his earthly sojourn is destined to be even more tortuous.

What, then, is the human task? With the abundant references to Qoheleth's melancholy outlook, which fill so many commentaries, one can lose sight of the important direction he gives. The book is part of Israel's Wisdom tradition; its insights eventually won it a place in the Hebrew canon. The order in which one finds himself cannot be discerned or mastered, but one can learn how to cope with it. The dim aspects of the book can be stressed to the point that its strong emphasis on the pleasures of life is lost sight of. These pleasures are meant to be enjoyed—pleasures of the body as well as the mind—just as suffering has to be endured. Therefore, one must take the joy of the moment and live it to the full; it, too, is part of the divine design. Where is the wisdom in trying to solve the "eternal questions," which result in frustration, if not ill health, as God-provided pleasures pass by unnoticed and unpursued? This is not a jump from pessimism to hedonism. It is a fact of life for which Qoheleth claims no responsibility. It is the one certainty about which there can be no question. Therefore, wisdom lies in directing one's path with serenity through this maze of perplexities, not failing to accept from God's hand the joys that will certainly be present.

As Walter Eichrodt notes, this humble resignation before the greatness of God, which escapes manipulation by human categories, is itself a form of worship. Undoubtedly, as in the case of Job, we would qualify Qoheleth considerably in view of a fuller revelation. But this does not make the book valueless if we are to take seriously the fact that it has been part of our religious patrimony for well over two thousand years. It has a wisdom all its own even though it severely tests the wisdom that preceded it. For our purposes, its importance for the problem of evil within an evolving process of reflection, is considerable, if for no other reason than that Qoheleth had the courage to say what many of his contemporaries may have only thought. The conclusions of a long-held position are educed, shown to be wanting and set aside. The traditional position of retribution has reached a watershed; it can go no further. In this sense Old Testament Wisdom would have been incomplete without Qoheleth. To a simplistic fundamentalism that sees the Old Testament as a revealed monolith, as simply the word of God without the give and take of evolving human thought, Qoheleth stands in clear opposition. He is the first to admit that there has been no answer to many of the questions he has raised in examples drawn from daily life. But as a citizen of his own age, with the limitations that revelation had thus far imposed, he had said as much as he could and we are struck by the forthrightness with which he says it.

The history of theology affords many examples of the tension between champions of the achieved position and promoters of "new frontiers." Post-exilic wisdom, as reflected in the canonical books themselves, has provided us with one of the most interesting examples. There is something timeless about this struggle between theory and actuality, especially when it touches such a raw nerve as the problem of evil and its consequences. It was a problem much too vital to be consigned to the dusty tomes of theoretical abstraction. It gives ample proof, if such be needed, that the Bible is indeed the word of God in the words of men.

IV.

EVIL AND THE FUTURE

Two principal reasons make eschatology important in any discussion of the problem of evil. The first is the inherent claim that in the final days Yahweh would dramatically intervene to crush the power of evil in the world. The second is because it was within the context of eschatology that the first notions of resurrection appear. It is this afterlife affirmation which provided a solution to the problem of retribution. Each of these areas merits our consideration.

Evil in the Old Testament is not an eternal force. There is no mythological dualism predicating the existence of evil as an integral component of the cosmos. Evil, in the sense of sin and its consequences, had a beginning, as impossible as it may have been to pinpoint in time; this is clearly the sense of the first three chapters of Genesis, as we have noted. Since it had a beginning there was no reason why evil should not have an end as well, and Old Testament eschatology has no hesitation in affirming it will.[1] When Israel first begins to speak of the **beaharit hayyamin,** or the end of days, it does so mainly along historical lines. The climax of history was to be part of history itself, thus geographically, chrono-

---

[1] For a fuller treatment of eschatology, cf. Kittel, G., **Theological Dictionary of the N.T.** (Grand Rapids, 1964), "Eschatos."

logically and politically discernible. This is not to say, however, that the processes of history were sufficient of themselves to bring it about. The End Time was not seen as a human construct or an historical evolution. Since it exceeded man's forces in its nature and scope, Yahweh's direct intervention was necessary to make it a reality. The disorders within Israel and among the nations would never be corrected by human effort; hence the final time was accurately termed the "Day of Yahweh." Yet this eschatological outlook, which characterized the pre-exilic period, remained recognizable, having a continuity with the historical past. This included such features as peace among nations, the religious fidelity of Israel, the message of Israel reaching the Gentiles. It is within this context that Old Testament messianism is situated, with the anointed descendant of David presiding over God's people (Cf., e.g., Is 9:2-7; 11:1-9). This was also seen as a period rich in the blessings of land and flock.

This same end of days, however, was to be preceded by the purge of evil, with divine retribution first settling accounts before peace and tranquility were enthroned. Consequently, the Day of Yahweh is depicted in frightening terms in what Amos calls "darkness, not light; gloom without a single ray of light" (Am 5:20). The nations were not to be spared either, least of all those which had subjected Israel to their tyranny (Cf. Am, ch. 1). Isaiah sees it as a day of woe for all proud men without distinction (Is 2:9-22), with Jeremiah viewing its internationalism in universal terms (Jr 25:14-38; chs. 46-51). In the main, this is the eschatology of the pre-exilic prophets delineated as a climax to history, effected by Yahweh himself bringing religious and social peace after the definitive eradication of evil.

Apocalyptic

Eschatology in the period after the exile moves in a different direction, giving rise to the literary genre known as apocalyptic, from the Greek **apokalypsis** (revelation). It continues the prophetic tradition while interpreting the present and future in distinctly new terms. The main difference lies in the fact that it does not operate along the historical lines of the past; that recognizable and familiar continuity between the new message and the past is no longer present. More than ever the inbreaking of Yahweh is necessary to fashion the future in ways which have the drastic and cosmic dimensions of the original act of creation. Rather than being in continuity with history, apocalyptic marks history's end. It is true that the historical often merges with the trans-historical; the political powers, for example, that beset the Jews at the time can be identified. But they have assumed a new dimension as the personification of evil. The denouement has also passed to another realm. Yahweh does not move through his people with their hopes and traditions in effecting his victory; rather he comes toward them in ways that are as startling as they are unpredictable. The emphasis is no longer on a destroyed Assyria or Babylon or on a faithful davidic monarch in a restored Jerusalem; it is now a cosmic destruction followed by a new creation presided over by its own heavenly retinue. Various reasons have been advanced for this change of emphasis. It may have arisen from dissatisfaction with the Israelite monarchy as the principal agent of the promise or the inability to foresee any historical solution after the bitter experience of the exile and the moral relapse that came in its wake. It may well be that Israel's moral and political helplessness precipitated apocalyptic. The fact is that it is a post-exilic phenomenon which colors much of biblical and extra-biblical literature through the intertestamental period into New Testament times.

Apocalyptic is so "unearthly" that even its language has to be deciphered. The final inbreaking is clearly God's, not only in the act itself but also in its announcement. Consequently, the "coded" message is received in vision and often accompanied by an angelic interpreter. This oblique way of communication assures its comprehension by the believer while leaving it obscure for the unbeliever. Symbolic language abounds in apocalyptic and it has proved to be the Waterloo of more than one school of biblical interpretation. The human body and its parts, animals, heavenly bodies, numbers—all take on a defined and precise meaning in describing the prelude to and the final event itself. Yet this does not make apocalyptic unintelligible and esoteric. Only when one lacks a knowledge of the historical period and its personalities which it reflects, or a knowledge of the Old Testament in general, where many of the images have been previously employed, is there a difficulty in interpretation. Unless the author had a message which he intended to be understood he would never have addressed himself to his contemporaries. In fact, where he feels his thought demands further clarity he supplies it through an interpreter or some other means. His symbolism is at times overstated to assure clear identification.

Once again, evil plays a vital role in the veiled message of apocalyptic, its defeat and the subsequent establishment of the Lord's reign being central to the genre. The final battle, taken over from the prophets, is now painted in transcendent and cosmic hues. Not only Israel and the nations are tainted by evil's presence but the entire created order. The universal upheaval to effect evil's demise is carried out and completed by

Yahweh himself without the instrumentality of human forces.

The clearest example of Old Testament apocalyptic appears in the book of Daniel.[2] Written between 167 and 164 B.C., Daniel springs from the period when Hellenistic imperialism was being exercised in Palestine by the dynasty of the Seleucids in the person of Antiochus IV Epiphanes. The hated Seleucids, in their attempts to Hellenize the Jews, were guilty of religious and moral atrocities which matched those of any previous occupying power. Bitter reaction eventually led to the Jewish revolt under the Maccabees, recounted in the two books bearing their name. The book of Daniel attempts to console the persecuted Jews in a series of stories and apocalyptic visions, literarily connected with a certain Daniel of the Babylonian exile. By this literary fiction the book can speak "prophetically" from a distance four centuries removed from the actual events in assuring the eventual vindication of God's people.

Chapters 7 to 12 contain Daniel's apocalypse. With the book written in the mid-sixties of the second century, much that is symbolically described in the fall of successive foreign dominators has already taken place. The four monsters (ch. 7) represent the Babylonians, the Medes, the Persians and the Greeks; all have become part of history by the time Daniel is composed. The very incarnation of evil, represented by various symbols in the Daniel apocalyptic, is Antiochus Epiphanes, appearing as the last beast's "little horn" (ch. 7 and 8). Antiochus is still active when Daniel is written (as is evident from his description in ch. 11), but his barbarous campaign against the Jews and their beliefs has made him the summary of all evil, the symbolic expression of the

---

(2) Other examples with varying degrees of applicability: Ez 38-39; Is 24-27; Zech 9-14.

whole force, a sign of the End Time. The stage is now set for final and universal retribution. In their persecuted state, the Jews themselves can offer little to victory; it must come from Yahweh himself who will then bring history to an end. It is this triumph that is described in the defeat of the symbolic beast, final resurrection and the liberation of the faithful of Israel, depicted as the Son of Man.

What is important to note is apocalyptic's strong affirmation that there can be no coexistence between Yahweh and evil. Its radical elimination is decreed as preliminary to the Kingdom's establishment. The force that was rather unobtrusively unleashed in Genesis and which has continued to take its toll in history must ultimately be defeated on a scale which has become all-encompassing. It is of such proportions that humanity is in no way equal to the task; Yahweh himself will do battle, with no doubt left as to who the victor will be.

The fact that the end did not come at the time nor in the way expected by the apocalypticists should not dull the cutting edge of their message. It should also caution us against too literal an interpretation or too facile an application of apocalyptic symbolism to other historical moments, past or present. The genre presents its basic theme of the eventual triumph of God over evil against the background of the troubled times in which the Jewish, or later Christian, community was living. The historical moment of trial had all the characteristics of eschatological tribulation and it was within that context that the end was envisioned. The fact that it proved not to be the historical moment is diminished in importance in view of the fact that the actual experience has passed into transcendent categories. Antiochus Epiphanes became a symbol of the great Evil which, regardless of when or how, will have to be vanquished before the end arrives. It is for this reason that Daniel, like the book of

Revelation in the New Testament, has won a permanent place in the collection of sacred writings, recognized as inspired. It is a mistake to look for a literal fulfillment of apocalyptic; it is equally wrong to see it merely as an historically conditioned expression which has no abiding value. The conflict between God and evil is too integral a datum of biblical revelation to permit its depiction in any form to be disregarded. The very nature of God demanded that the problem of evil be resolved in Jewish and Christian eschatology. Therein lies the permanent vitality of apocalyptic.

Immortality

It is in the same second century book of Daniel that afterlife sanctions become a clear datum of Old Testament revelation. When the "time" of the dominance of the great pagan kings has been completed and the era of persecution has passed, the just shall be delivered and those who have fallen in death shall also be vindicated.

> At that time there shall arise
> Michael, the great prince,
> guardian of your people;
> It shall be a time unsurpassed in distress
> since nations began until that time.
> At that time your people shall escape,
> everyone who is found written in the book.
> Many of those who sleep
> in the dust of the earth shall awake;
> Some shall live forever, others
> shall be an everlasting horror and disgrace.
> But the wise shall shine brightly
> like the splendor of the firmament
> And those who lead the many to justice
> shall be like the stars forever (Dn 12:1-3).

The text must be viewed in context. It is not a treatise on the general resurrection of the dead; it is concerned with the final lot of the persecuted Jews as well as those who had died theretofore. At that time the just or predestined (whose names are in the book of life) escape the lot of the vanquished persecutors and evildoers. With reference to the dead the text simply states that due retribution will be meted out to them as well, envisioning a resurrection of the just to eternal splendor. The lot of the evil is not that clear. Do they also rise before being consigned to permanent desolation? Such would seem to be the sense, with the "some" and the "others" (literally, in the Hebrew, "these". . ."those") being comprised in the "many" (v. 2).[3]

Thus, the resurrection, though viewed restrictively, is admitted in principle. In keeping with traditional Hebrew anthropology, it is a resurrection of the body-person. Since the life principle animates a body from which it is then functionally inseparable, there is no question of future life being reserved for a detached self-contained principle as the soul. It would be incorrect to speak of a "resurrection of the body," such implying hylomorphic categories alien, at least at this point, to Jewish thought. No lasting joy, or punishment for that matter, could be envisioned which did not include the total person. Daniel says nothing about the exact nature of this resurrected life; there is no attempt to specify eternal joy or sorrow.

It is hard to avoid the question as to why the notion of eternal sanctions appears so late in the development of Old Testament thought. At any earlier stage was it

---

(3) The possible reference to resurrection in Is 26:19, contained in the "little apocalypse" of Is 24-27, also a post-exilic composition, is not as clear as Dn. It may have symbolic reference to Israel's national rebirth (cf. Ez 37).

in the interests of avoiding comparisons with Egyptian afterlife thought which, in its simple prolongation of present existence, was seen as inadequate? Was the very idea of resurrection mistrusted because of the part it played in the Near Eastern mythology of dying and rising gods? Did it need the catalyst of Greek thought for the concept to mature? Speculation has looked in these and other directions for an answer. Perhaps we shall never have a certain explanation. That it represents a new departure in biblical teaching on retribution is undeniable. We are forced to restrict ourselves to the data on the subject which the Bible itself affords.

Resurrection appears also in the second book of Maccabees dating about 100 B.C. As the mother of the narrative (ch. 7) sees her sons tortured and killed for their determination not to abandon their faith, each son in turn gives expression to his convictions, climactically affirming that the Lord will ultimately be their vindicator. They are ready to die rather than violate the Law (7:2), thus assuring mercy before the divine tribunal (7:6). There is utter confidence in the future, once the ordeal is passed: ". . . the King of the world will raise us up to live again forever. It is for his laws that we are dying" (7:9). For the wicked there can be no resurrection unto life (7:14); for them and their descendants there can only be torment (7:17). Suffering is seen to have an atoning value for sins committed (7:18-19); moreover, the death of the just can have the force of expiatory prayer on behalf of the guilty (7:37-38).

Later in the same book of Maccabees, Judas discovers pagan amulets, forbidden by the Jews, on the bodies of his fallen troops. In the interest of their participation in the resurrection of the dead he has an expiatory sacrifice offered in Jerusalem on their behalf (12:38-46). The passage is noteworthy not only for its clear statement of belief in the resurrection but also for its expressed conviction that guilt could be erased even for the dead through the prayers of the living.

The book of Wisdom, a Greek composition, marks the **terminus ad quem** of Old Testament sapiential literature and was written by an Alexandrian Jew at the turn of the last century before Christ. Although a devout Yahwist, he is anything but a stranger to the advanced Hellenistic thought which surrounded the Jews in the Egyptian diaspora. He attempts something of a synthesis with Greek culture, in reaffirming the perennial validity of Yahwistic wisdom in the face of the new thought by using concepts which owe their origin, in many instances, to the same philosophical world. Thus, while Wisdom is a personified attribute of God himself, her qualities of intelligence, multiformity and all-pervasiveness (7:22-8:1) are shared by the Greek **Nous** or world soul. Solomon, to whom parts of the book are given literary attribution, is presented as endowed with gifts which go far beyond the practical insights attributed to him by earlier wisdom and are better suited to the philosopher of a later time.

> For he (God) gave me sound knowledge of existing things, that I might know the organization of the universe and the force of its elements.
>
> The beginning and the end and the midpoint of time, the changes in the sun's course and the variations of the seasons.
>
> Cycles of years, positions of the stars, natures of animals, tempers of beasts,
>
> Powers of the winds and thoughts of men, uses of plants and virtues of roots—
>
> Such things as are hidden I learned, and such as are plain;

for Wisdom, the artificer of all, taught me
(7:17-22).

The weight of Wisdom's effort is to encourage the
faithful Jew by showing that the authentic wisdom has
not been lost despite the waves of sophisticated pagan
thought which have inundated him. The author returns
to the clear evidence of Yahweh's superior wisdom in
citing, for example, the historic defeat of Egyptian cun-
ning at the time of the Exodus, while taking daring steps
to show that there are features of the "contemporary"
philosophy that can bolster the Jews' traditional faith.
He is evidently concerned about those who are wavering
in their beliefs as well as those who had already abandoned them. It is also at least likely that he is interested
in correcting attitudes among his non-Jewish contemporaries about the imagined primitive, if not barbaric,
content of Hebrew thought by competing with them on
their own grounds.

In short, while discussion will continue on the extent
to which Wisdom has drawn on Hellenistic thought, with
which it was evidently well versed, it is hardly imagin-
able that it could have come from any milieu other than
that to which biblical scholarship has attributed it.
There was a time when Christian thought was uncom-
fortable with the prospect of inspired writings, the source
of divine revelation, being in some way indebted to philosophical findings which are the result of merely human
skills. It cannot be doubted that revelation and human
reason are distinct spheres. Yet, today more than ever,
we realize how difficult it is to separate them into neat,
easily distinguishable categories. Admittedly, it is more
difficult in some cases than others but the problem remains. The mode of God's communicating himself to
man is varied; it is not necessarily a process which passes
through one conduit only. We should not be surprised if

the encounter between Hebrew Yahwism and Greek philosophy proved to enrich the former, even in books which we recognize as inspired. The one God is not restricted by the categories which we might impose in speaking in various and sundry ways to the creation which is the work of his hands.

Nowhere has this thesis been more exhaustively discussed than with reference to Wisdom's unequivocal affirmation of immortality. In encouraging the Jews of his time, the author addresses himself to the evident prosperity of the wicked. With a dispatch that by-passes centuries of argumentation, he summarily dismisses the problem. Such prosperity is only apparent and transitory at best; in the light of immortality, sanctions are eternal. In contrast to the just who are destined for eternal splendor, the wicked, God "shall strike down, speechless and prostrate, and rock them to their foundations." Their only lot is that of "dishonored corpses" (4:19). Wisdom sees the future which lies beyond this fleeting life as determining the meaning of suffering and joy, as well as sin and virtue, in the context of daily experience. In dealing with these burning issues he has room to move in a way which was denied the greater number of his predecessors.

To what extent did Greek thinking on the soul's immortality influence this breakthrough in Jewish thought? It is unquestionable that the author of Wisdom was aware of the body-soul distinction which, as has been noted, did not play a part in Hebrew anthropology. He states that the "corruptible body burdens the soul" (9:15); the human composite is one of clay and a soul "on loan" eventually to be given back (15:8). However, it is more than a question of particular texts; the Alexandrian milieu of pagan wisdom conditioned much of the outlook of the author. It is clear that these are categories with which he is conversant, even when he finds its conclusions wanting. In approaching the current philosophy, as friend or foe, it is evident that he is no stranger to it and does not assume an outsider's position.

Yet, when it comes to immortality, Wisdom does not base his affirmation on the soul but rather on moral uprightness. It is virtue or, more precisely, justice, that leads to eternal life. This is not the lot of the wicked for whom immortality, in Wisdom's sense, is impossible. Rather, "the just live forever, and in the Lord is their recompense, and the thought of them is with the Most High" (5:15). In a key passage it is stated:

> To know you (God) well is complete justice
> and to know your might is the root of im-
> mortality (15:3).

To know or experience God is to live a life in accordance with his will to the exclusion of the death-inducing forces of sin. This is justice as found in man. But the experience of God is also to know his creative force before which death itself (16:13) as well as Sheol (17:14) are powerless. Therefore, it is the person who lives in accord with dictates of a God powerful enough to subdue death and all its consequences that will live forever. Moreover, justice, as an attribute of God himself, is by its very nature immortal (1:15) and man's participation in it is his principal claim to an unending future. It is this combination of God's might and man's justice, rather than anything inherent in human nature itself, on which Wisdom bases its teaching on immortality.[4]

There is no mention of a future resurrection in Wisdom. Such an idea had no currency in the Greek world and this may explain, at least in part, its absence. Yet,

---

(4) Murphy, R. E., "To know your might is the root of immortality," Cath. Bib. Quart., 25 (Jan. 1963), 88-93.

the blessedness of the world to come, as found in Wisdom, has elements in common with developments in Jewish belief. While it does not state that the body will participate in this blessedness (nor, at the same time, does it exclude it), Wisdom does speak of this future lot as being a share in that of the "holy ones," "the sons of God," who comprise the heavenly court (5:5). On this point authors have pointed out the resemblance between Wisdom and the Essene literature from the Dead Sea, the product of an important segment of pre-Christian Judaism.

In a hymn appended to the Qumran community's Manual of Discipline, God's chosen ones, endowed with virtue and knowledge described as a "fount of righteousness," have been given an inheritance with the "Sons of Heaven" (IQS 11:7-8). Elsewhere, the purified sinner is presented as given a place "in the host of the holy beings, and brought into communion with the Sons of Heaven" (IQH 3:19-23). The parallel with Wisdom is evident. It is uprightness of life that serves as the link which assimilates the just to the angels. Thus, in addition to justice itself, it is the notion of the heavenly angelic body which can be said to find its earthly counterpart in the liturgical assembly at Qumran, that provides the positive content to late Judaism's speculations on immortality. The just man can be said to pass from an earthly choir, hymning God's praises, to a heavenly one. Again, this is not derived from philosophical speculation on the spiritual nature of man nor, for that matter, that of the angels either. It is basically a question of an eternal heavenly body with which the just man has the right of eventual association.

The consequences of Wisdom's immortality on the centuries-old problem of retribution are incalculable. Eternal sanctions make the difference. Ironically, it is the evildoers who now justify their wrongdoing on the basis of the limitations imposed by the traditional position. Since death is terminal, blotting out even the memory of one's name, there remains only the present which must be turned to one's profit.

> Come, therefore, let us enjoy the good
> things that are real . . .
> Let us have our fill of costly wine and
> perfumes . . .
> Let us oppress the needy just man;
> Let us neither spare the widow . . .
> But let our strength be our norm of justice;
> for weakness proves itself useless (2:6, 7, 10-11).

Such a "might makes right" philosophy would never have won the approval of the traditionalists; they would have found such conclusions abhorrent. Even opponents of the conservative stand were not so audacious; Qoheleth may have counselled the enjoyment of the God-given pleasures of this world but he never counselled immorality. Yet, by such a juxtaposition, the inadequacy of the former position is given full play. In fact, in justifying their illicit activity, the wicked mouth the teaching of the past in words which bear more than a passing resemblance to the laments of Job and Qoheleth:

> Brief and troublesome is our lifetime;
> neither is there any remedy for man's dying,
> Nor is anyone known to have come
> back from the nether world . . .
> Because the breath in our nostrils is a smoke and
> reason is a spark at the beating of our hearts,
> And when this is quenched, our body will be
> ashes and our spirit will be poured abroad like
> unresisting air . . . For our lifetime is the

passing of a shadow; and our dying cannot be
deferred because it is fixed with a seal and
no one returns (2:1-3, 5).

With immortality now a datum, Wisdom confronts
the old problems with new insight. The "curse" of child-
lessness is not the consequence of sin, nor does it doom
its victim to the lot of a community outsider. What is all
important is the virtue of the childless one. For she who
is "childless and undefiled . . . shall bear fruit at the visi-
tation of souls" (3:13). So also the eunuch, guilty of no
misdeed, "shall be given fidelity's choice reward and a
more gratifying heritage in the Lord's temple" (3:14).
An early and untimely death, another nerve center of
the traditional position, is now seen in a totally new light.
Old age does not of itself prove anything, despite Proverb's dictum that "gray hair is a crown of glory and is
gained by virtuous living" (16:31). Wisdom tells us:

> . . . the just man though he die early shall
> be at rest,
> For the age that is honorable comes
> not with the passing of time,
> nor can it be measured in terms of years.
> Rather, understanding is the hoary crown for
> men, and an unsullied life, the attainment
> of old age (4:7-9).

In fact, the young person's death may be a sign of divine
favor in being snatched away from the moral dangers
of life before they can take their toll of his innocence
(4:10f). In all of this, we are faced with distinctly new
perspectives. Wisdom recognizes that the just still suffer
and the enigma cannot be completely resolved. But he
takes up the theme of trial and purification which, in the
light of immortality, becomes more understandable.

But the souls of the just are in the hand of God.
For if before men, indeed, they be punished
yet is their hope full of immortality;
Chastised a little, they shall be greatly blessed
because God tried them and found them
worthy of himself.
As gold in the furnace, he proved them and as
sacrificial offerings he took them to himself
(3:1, 4-6).

Centuries passed between the earliest Israelite sages
who wrestled with the problem of evil and the developed
climate of thought which produced the book of Wisdom.
The evolution has been so pronounced that one might
easily wonder where the former stand with reference to
the latter within the Old Testament compendium. It is
impossible to gloss over Wisdom's comment on the reasoning of the wicked (ch. 2), cited earlier, wherein it is
stated that, in their failure to recognize man's imperish-
able character, their conclusions are simply erroneous
(2:21-23). Are we not compelled logically to say the same
of a considerable body of Old Testament material contained in books which are purportedly "inerrant"? Perhaps nothing shows so graphically the inadequacy of an
earlier position on the inerrancy of the Scriptures understood in fundamentalist terms. A position not without its
modern adherents, there is an immense danger, not to
mention folly, in lifting passages from the sacred text and
endowing them with an immutable and absolute verity
because "God is their author." If today revelation itself is
seen in an organic sense, accommodated to man's ability
to understand, and covering centuries of development and
refinement, the same is equally true in any considerations of inerrancy. This is not to say that the early teaching on retribution had no element of truth; its truth was
proportionate to its capacity of expression. It was as true

as Israel's ability to understand the divine design at a given moment in history could be. But when we speak of the Bible's inerrancy on the question of retribution, to limit ourselves to our present concern, it is of the Scriptures as a whole that we speak. Particular parts can be said to participate in that inerrancy to the extent that they contribute to the teaching in its entirety. We cannot fault biblical authors for not arriving at conclusions beyond the insights they had, nor are we justified in making them say any more than they did.

In a particular way, the post-exilic period in Israel's history was marked by theological pluralism. There were diverse attitudes on law and cult; there was a particularism which was opposed by universalism; certain canonical books are counter-checks on others; the entire question of retribution went through a process of lengthy refinement. There were a variety of theologies at work and they are reflected in the Old Testament literature. Only a maximalist view, which sees the Old Testament solely in terms of its revealed, and therefore divine, content has any difficulty with this. The fact is that in its diversity and contrast, it says much about "the depth of the riches and the wisdom and the knowledge of God" (Rm 11:33), which a chosen people, with the light given to them, strove to plummet, if not always infallibly, at least unfalteringly.

Redemptive Suffering

There are chronological arguments which militate against treating Isaiah's Songs of the Servant at the conclusion of our Old Testament considerations on the problem of evil. These four songs are found in the exilic and post-exilic sections of Isaiah and, in the consensus of biblical scholars today, are to be distinguished from the earlier half of the book which, in the main, is a pre-exilic composition.[5] As part of what is generally called "Second Isaiah" (chs. 40-55), the songs represent those new aspirations which came from the purifying experience of the Exile and can be clearly distinguished thematically from the oracles of the original prophet Isaiah. We are accustomed today to speak of an Isaian school which perpetuated the teaching of Isaiah and applied it to Israel's situation at later significant moments. While discussion continues to center around a more exact dating of the Songs, since they are inserted into the body of chapters 40-55, even an outside date of the mid-fifth century would require that their insights into suffering precede that of such late compositions as Maccabees and Wisdom.

The Suffering Servant is treated here because of its singular and distinctive approach to the value of human tragedy. Regardless of when the Songs were composed, their emphasis on suffering as vicarious never became normative in later thought. In this sense they stand apart, as startling and unresolved as the figure of the Servant himself. Not written in the midst of the heated polemic over the traditional views on retribution, the Songs can be treated separately without losing sight of the important light that suffering for others casts on the entire question. They are also treated at this point because they represent an important prelude to the New Testament. While the central figure of the Isaian Songs has not been identified to the unanimous, or even quasi-unanimous, satisfaction of Old Testament scholars, the New Testament itself does not hesitate to see Jesus as the Servant. There is no doubt that the New Testament authors, and

---

(5) Thus chapters 1-39 (with some important exceptions) contain oracles of the eighth-century prophet; Second Isaiah (chs. 40-55) depicts the return from the Babylonian exile in the sixth century; Third Isaiah (chs. 56-66), distinct in vocabulary and perspective from the former, was probably composed after resettlement in Palestine.

particularly the evangelists, make this identification, although not a few New Testament scholars argue that in the course of his earthly ministry it was Christ himself who gradually came to speak of his salvific mission in terms of the Servant model. Regardless of how the author of the Songs may have envisioned the eventual actualization of his message, the striking parallels between the protagonist and the person of Jesus exist, especially in terms of the atoning death.

The four Songs interrupt the continuity of Second Isaiah, a factor which led Bernard Duhm in 1892 to isolate them from the rest of the text. While it is true that their removal does nothing to alter the basic outline of the book, this is not to say that the poems constitute a unity among themselves. There is certainly the thread of a basic theme but it would exceed the evidence to consider them an original literary unit. For our purposes it is important to trace the dramatic evolution of the Servant's career as it emerges in the detached poems.

Yahweh himself introduces the Servant in the first Song (Is 42:1-4). He is given a prophetic mission to establish the Lord's justice, not in Israel, but among the nations. Not a Messianic ruler nor invincible warrior, he will achieve his goal with calm conviction, respect, even gentleness—a spirit that is opposed to violence. The description is brief but, in its character delineation, strongly related to the Servant's eventual lot. The second Song (Is 49:1-6) is autobiographical. The Servant speaks, with shades of Jeremiah, of his divine designation, a vocation which reaches back to his mother's womb. His role as an agent of salvation to the Gentiles remains intact but Israel, too, is to benefit by his work. He will effect a conversion of Jacob to the Lord, a necessary concomitant feature of Old Testament universalism. In verse 3 he is called "Israel," a designation not without difficulty in terms of the Servant's identity, requiring that any solution recognize that the Servant is both an expression of Israel and one who works for Israel. In this second Song, the drama has moved forward. The central figure has already experienced frustration in his efforts; opposition has surfaced in ways which remain unspecified.

> Though I thought I had toiled in vain,
> and for nothing, uselessly, spent my strength,
> Yet my reward is with the Lord,
> my recompense is with my God (49:4).

The spirit of hostility to the Servant has become more intense in the third Song (50:4-9); the hero is sustained only by his unwavering confidence in the Lord. He speaks of persecution and violence in words which, in the vividness of poetic expression, only underscore the atmosphere of animosity which surrounds him. True to the character description of the first Song, the Servant does not respond in kind. He does not resist the evil but submits with patience, fully confident of his ultimate vindication. But the question comes to the fore: What is the specific task of the Servant? The text is silent about the cause of his rejection and focuses on what he was called to endure. His experience is not unlike that of the prophets, yet with certain important and, at this point, inexplicable differences.

It is the fourth Song (52:13-53:12), that brings the drama to its climax. Yahweh is the first speaker (52:13-15), stating that the Servant's final vindication will be as startling as his previous stricken state. The latter, in traditional terms, would have been seen as clear indication of sinfulness. A chorus of his contemporaries, seemingly fellow Israelites, recounts the pitiful state to which the Servant has been brought (53:1-10). Unimpressive in appearance, rejected by his peers, subjected to mental and physical abuses, he suffers with resignation and silence. Eventually brought to his death, he is consigned to the oblivion of the pit. But the marvel of his peers arises from their realization that this was, in fact, the significance of his mission. The Servant was innocent. This death was redemptive. He atoned for the sins of others.

> Yet it was our infirmities that he bore,
> our sufferings that he endured,
> While we thought of him as stricken,
> as one smitten by God and afflicted.
> But he was pierced for our offenses,
> crushed for our sins;
> Upon him was the chastisement that makes us whole,
> by his stripes we were healed.
> We had all gone astray like sheep,
> each following his own way;
> But the Lord laid upon him
> the guilt of us all (53:4-6).

Because of his voluntary and vicarious suffering on behalf of "the many," the Servant is finally vindicated by the Lord. In some undefined way he triumphs over death and the fruits of his suffering are made available to the guilty. It exceeds the evidence to see this as a pledge of the protagonist's personal resurrection. Such might well be the case if the Servant were to be seen as a specific individual. Many critics recognize the strongly personal lines in which the person and career of the Servant are etched but they are cognizant as well of the collective features of his personality. He is called "Israel" once in the Songs, just as Israel is designated as the Lord's Servant several times in Second Isaiah.

In addition, the question of personal resurrection

hinges on whether or not the Servant, even if he is viewed as an individual, is seen as an actual historical person. The whole discussion remains very open. However, it is possible to see the Servant as an idealized future personality who embodies the best of Israel, past and present. He is an individual who represents a collectivity, as in the case of patriarchal personalities, e.g., Jacob and Esau. As John McKenzie notes: "The Servant is conceived as an individual figure, but he is the figure who recapitulates in himself all the religious gifts and the religious mission of Israel."[6] As representative of the faithful Israel the Servant is personally concretized, but that is not to say that the author necessarily posits the eventual appearance of an historical person that will fit the role. What the author does maintain is the eventual salvation of the broader Israel and the nations through vicarious atonement.

Despite the vivid presentation of the Servant's suffering, the actual mode in which this deliverance will be realized remains unknown. The same is true of his ultimate triumph. The notion of resurrection is not actually stated; that the Servant will see the results of his mission is. But at this point to what extent is the idea of the continuation of the faithful Israel dominant in the author's thought? Have we gone much beyond Ezechiel's resurrected "dry bones," which is unquestionably a reference to the new Israel?

The Songs of the Servant are full of hope for a sinful and repentant Israel, as well as for the nations. In their sinful state they are powerless to effect their redemption; such must come from another source. From the abiding faithful element in Israel's midst, perhaps best identified with the Old Testament "remnant," selfless

------

(6) McKenzie, J. L., Second Isaiah (Anchor Bible), Doubleday, N. Y, 1968, p. L111.

dedication and generosity of spirit will realize a vicarious atonement. The description of this event is not done in broad strokes but in precise lines centered around the concrete person of the innocent Servant. This is as much as the evidence permits us to say.

It is not the identity of the Servant, however, that is our principal concern, but rather the aspect of his suffering. In the reaction of the onlookers to the drama, we remain in the traditional mold of thought. The Servant suffers because he is a sinner, one rejected by God. Their observation differs little from that of Job's friends. This solution is, however, clearly rejected. It does not tally with experience since he "had done no wrong, nor spoken any falsehood" (53:9). But more importantly, it passes from consideration because of a revelation which leaves nations startled and kings speechless (52:15). Evil is inflicted and endured, not because of personal guilt nor in the interests of testing or purification, but for the sake of the sin-ridden who in their obstinacy are powerless to help themselves. It remains for them to recognize such selfless love and appropriate its fruits in repentance and reconciliation.

In many respects the idea is novel in Israelite thought. It remains undeveloped even after Second Isaiah. Its importance forces us to ask how such a conclusion was reached, even while recognizing its revelatory and inspired character. Its origins may be found in the early idea of the "remnant" of Israel, the conviction that Yahweh's punitive action was never total. Fidelity to his promises precluded complete annihilation. Through repeated invasions and destruction, the faithful Israelites had suffered with their compatriots but had ultimately been delivered. They were thus enabled to be the messengers of an undying hope, the consolers of a sinful and downtrodden people. In a certain sense, they had suffered in the interests of others. It should be remembered that the Servant Songs are the fruit of the painful experience of the Babylonian Exile. A constant theme of Second Isaiah is the emergence from suffering of a new and faithful people, destined to resettle their homeland and rebuild their temple. Such an experience could have provided the fertile soil out of which the theology of the Servant emerged. This is not to deprive the Songs of their unique contribution. The "remnant" theology had never articulated a correlation between suffering and mission. The preservation of a faithful Israel benefitted a sinful people but the "remnant" did not atone for the wrongdoing of the past. It provided a hope for the future; it did not eradicate the evil that had transpired. In the case of the Servant we have a victim—in sacrificial language an **asam** or guilt offering (53:10)—one who assumes the guilt of others in order that it may be removed. The record of "the many" before God is rectified through the suffering of one.

The theology of the Servant has given an added dimension to the role of suffering in the salvation of Israel. It is more than something simply to be endured in the interests of a greater good; it has a redemptive value hinging, of course, on sentiments of self-dedication to Yahweh's will. It is still sin that is the ultimate cause of suffering, but the inevitable link between cause and effect in individual terms has been broken. Charity can transfer the weight of sin to another's shoulders; faith and repentance can make the transfer effective in the sinner's life. It is an insight that goes no further in the Old Testament.[7] Perhaps the passage was too full of

---

(7) 2 M 7:37ff. is, at best, a weak echo of vicarious atonement. The last son offers his life that the persecution of his people may end (and its persecutors be punished!). Nothing explicit is said about the atoning value of death; in fact, the people have been paying the price of their sin in persecution (cf.v.38).

mystery to become normative; the Servant, too singular in his dedication to admit of any broad application. And yet the teaching stands with unmistakable clarity. Through an acceptance of suffering, in even succumbing to its direct consequences, victory is achieved. And this is done, not for self, but for others, who, despite their evil ways, will have the ability to see its meaning and make its gains their own.

V.

THE FULLNESS OF TIME

At that time, some were present who told him about the Galileans whose blood Pilate had mixed with their sacrifices. He said in reply: "Do you think that these Galileans were the greatest sinners in Galilee just because they suffered this? By no means! But I tell you, you will all come to the same end unless you reform. Or take those eighteen who were killed by a falling tower in Siloam. Do you think they were more guilty than anyone else who lived in Jerusalem? Certainly not! But I tell you, you will all come to the same end unless you reform (Lk 13:1-5).

In speaking of the problem of retribution in the New Testament, (especially in the Gospels), we are speaking of a span of time which covered the entire first century, during which period Christian thought was in evolution. The teaching of Jesus passed into the life of the early Church where it underwent adaptation and application in the light of changing times and circumstances. This evolution is reflected in the canonical Gospels and can be seen in the other New Testament writings as well, especially in the epistles of Paul. Our study of the Old Testament has made us accustomed to such development. While the composition of the New

Testament covers a much shorter period of time, the same factor is nonetheless at work. As in the Old Testament, there are different theologies present in the New Testament through which the teaching of Jesus is refracted.

The above-cited dialogue from Jesus' ministry, as recounted in Luke's gospel, serves more than one important function in illustrating early Christianity's outlook on retribution. First of all, it indicates that the traditional position which links tragedy with wrongdoing had not been preempted by the belief in future sanctions during the time of Jesus' ministry. In fact, the Sadducees, the more conservative religious party among the Jews, adhered to the older Hebrew tradition and did not accept more recent developments on future life sanctions as final resurrection (Mt 22:23-24; Ac 23:6ff.). The fact that some Galileans and Jerusalemites had met such a fate could have been popularly construed as their "just due," a mentality with which we are already quite familiar. Secondly, Jesus moves the whole question of retribution to another plane. Sanctions are still an integral part of divine justice but their main manifestation will come at the time of final judgment.

In this light the story moves toward its main point: an appeal for conversion in view of the forthcoming trial. Jesus does not say that the victims of the recent tragedies were not guilty of evil; the point is simply not pertinent to his argument. His hearers were quite right in believing that God does punish, but they were in no position to play the role of arbiters. Divine justice cannot be reduced to a simple quid-pro-quo formula; only in the light of a future eschatological moment will the results of human justice and injustice become clear.

What is the judgment to which Luke alludes? In the preaching of Jesus himself, as well as John the Baptist before him, it referred to the final in-breaking of the

Kingdom of God, which lay at the heart of Old Testament hope, when evil would be definitively vanquished and full justice restored. It obviously entailed the separation of the virtuous from the evildoers for eternal bliss and condemnation respectively. In the light of contemporary understanding of the various levels of Gospel composition, it is reasonable to propose that in the actual ministry of Jesus, the exact mode of the Kingdom's coming was left largely undefined. As Luke would be using the episode, as well as the early Church from which he drew it, the emphasis would be falling on the return of Christ in glory as judge of the living and the dead, the time of the Parousia. It is for such a moment that even Christians themselves must live in a state of ongoing reform or conversion.

Nowhere are the **apriori** conclusions of the traditional view more categorically disavowed than in Luke's parable of Lazarus and the Rich Man (16:19-31). The lot of the grovelling poor man is in no way a consequence of his personal comportment, any more than the luxurious affluence of the Rich Man is a proof of his virtuous life. It is eternal sanctions, part and parcel of the Christian message from the beginning, which make the difference. The contrast arising from the reversed roles after death gives the story a poignant significance. Parenthetically, it is interesting to note that the desperate end of the Rich Man is not due to the evil which he did but the good which he failed to do. This is wholly in accord with the New Testament ethic which identifies sin, not solely with morally evil action but, more importantly, with the refusal to respond to a higher order of positive good, which includes social responsibility. It is on this basis that final sanctions will be meted out (Mt 25:31-46).

End time retribution is variously described in the synoptic Gospels as connected with the final entrance of God in history. It should be noted, however, that within the early Church, the cradle of the Gospels, the End Time is not reserved exclusively for the future; it is already inaugurated in the death and resurrection of Christ. For those who adhere to Christ and his message, the Kingdom is already present, with its final stage yet to be revealed. Therefore, it would be incorrect to read references to the inheritance of the Kingdom (or its loss) solely in future terms. It is important to keep the dual perspective of present and future in mind with the accent falling, at various times, more heavily on one or another. At any rate, sanctions are spoken of as a "great reward in heaven" (Mt 5:12), "partaking of the banquet in the Kingdom of God" (Lk 13:29), or "taking possession of the Kingdom prepared" (Mt 25:34). The fact that the Kingdom is seen as inaugurated in stages posits reward even in the present life, even though its content will be more spiritual than Old Testament categories permitted. There is promise of the hundredfold on this side of eternity, as well as life everlasting, for those who accept the Christian challenge. The same is true with regard to punishment. The scene of separation of good and bad in Matthew's judgment scene (25:31-46) looks to the final condemnation of the evildoer, but frequently in the first Gospel, as well as the other synoptics, present life sanctions are evident as well. The historical failure of the Jews to recognize the Kingdom's coming is the sin which results in their here-and-now exclusion. While the Gentiles flock to take their place with Abraham, Isaac and Jacob, the "natural heirs of the Kingdom will be driven out into the dark" (Mt 8:12). In Jeremiah-like tones, the destruction of Jerusalem and its temple is seen as retribution for the Jews' hardness of heart when faced with the call of Jesus (Mt 22:7).

It is this realization that final retribution resolves many unanswered questions which allows the first Gospel its latitude in accounting for both good and evil within the Church. In the parable of the weeds and the wheat growing up together, they are left untouched until the harvest (Mt 13:24-30). The kingdom of God is further described as a net thrown into the lake, drawing up everything within its sphere. This represents no problem since there will be a final "sorting out" at the end of time (Mt 13:47-49). The presence of the saint and the sinner within a religious society is perhaps so well confirmed by experience that it comes as no surprise and the Matthaean parables can be read today with little difficulty. It was not that easily understood in early Christian life which had its roots in a very ancient Hebrew separatism. It is sufficient to compare the early Church with the Essene community at Qumran where there was place only for the "elect" and from which the sinner was explicitly excluded.

The eschatological perspective of the synoptics, like that of the early Pauline epistles, is that of an earthly consummation, marked by the Lord's return, at which time the just would be brought into eternal communion with God. This is seen in terms of resurrection, since Old Testament categories are still operative which do not envision a detached spirit destined for final happiness (or condemnation), but rather the entire body person. Very much in line with what Wisdom has advanced, the inherent title to eternal sanctions is not the soul but the quality of one's life. It is those who adhere to Christ and his teaching that will be saved. This is true especially for Paul and the Gospel of John, regardless of whatever philosophical insight may have served as a catalyst to their thinking. It is those who have died to the flesh and now live in the Spirit (Paul) or those who participate in that new Life which is eternal (John) that are immortal. For Paul and John the continuity between the present and future states is so marked by this life in the Spirit it can be affirmed that eternity has already begun. In

this realized eschatology, Baptism represents the major
transition, wherein death is experienced and a new life
begun, thus reducing physical death to insignificance.

As long as the Parousia was seen as imminent, this
transition from the present life to the next represented
no major problem. Even those who died in the meantime
would rise in accord with their due precedence (1 Th
4:15ff.), clothed with the new "spiritual" body (1 Cor
15:35-44), at which time the living, properly transformed,
would also take their place. With the passing of time and
the Parousia's delay, there was more interest in the
interim state of the departed just. But in this regard it
must be admitted that the New Testament offers little
to satisfy our interest. There are, at best, oblique references to the interim period in Paul (2 Cor 5:1-5; Ph 1:
21ff.). The allusions are not uncontested by a number of
important Pauline scholars but, even with the admission
that Paul has come to reckon with a period of time before
the resurrection during which he will be "with Christ,"
there is no elaboration of its nature which, certainly
for Paul, without the transformed body would be incomplete and transitory. In John, the problem does not
appear; the only states of being that have meaning are
those of life and death, light and darkness. Both have
their beginning now and an unbroken continuity with
the future. Final resurrection remains a datum, but it is
neither proximate nor a dominant factor in the fourth
Gospel. The one who chooses life is destined to see it
continue without interruption; the same is true in the
choice of death. Physical death serves only to seal the
choice of the evildoer; judgment has already taken place
(Jn 3:18ff.; 5:24).

Does this mean, then, that in New Testament terms
the nexus between sin, suffering and death has dis-
appeared? The response is in the negative even while
it must be affirmed that the categories are more broadly

drawn. The fact that the connection was too narrow in much of the Old Testament did not vitiate its basic validity. The relationship between sin and suffering in general terms, which devolved from Genesis itself, finds a prominent place in the Gospel narratives. Human maladies, cosmic disorders and death, with mythical overtones that have an Old Testament ring, are all part of Satan's domain.

The Miracles

Recent Gospel scholarship has taken a new look at the miracles of Jesus and sees their significance as strongly related to this basic thesis.[1] One of the dominant beliefs of Old Testament eschatology centered around the final overthrow of evil prior to the Kingdom's definitive establishment. In apocalyptic imagery, as we have seen. this often takes the form of a pitched battle which reaches beyond Israel's traditional foes to touch the outer limits of the cosmos as well as the mythological sea monsters in the deeps of the ocean (e.g., Is 24-27). Wherever the presence of evil has been experienced, whether in ways that are real or imagined, battle is done to eliminate its activity and influence; only then can the reign of good and peace be introduced. It is against this background that literary and form critical studies view the Gospel miracles. Contrary to a rather widespread understanding, miracles were not performed by Jesus to assert Messianic or, much less, divine claims, on his behalf; the weight of the Gospel materials indicates that such claims were studiously avoided by Christ. What Jesus was doing (and the early Church, understanding) was proclaiming

---

(1) Cf. Richardson, A., The Miracle-Stories of the Gospels, SCM Press, London, 1972; Brown, R., "The Gospel Miracles" in The Bible in Current Catholic Thought. Herder, N. Y., 1962 (J. McKenzie, ed.)

the Kingdom's inauguration in his work and mission.

Christ does battle with evil in the person of Satan, its principal protagonist. The concept of a personal evil power, hostile to God and man and actively engaged in extending the reign of sin, is an important datum of the New Testament. It is, however, a relatively late development in biblical thought. As we have noted earlier, the Satan of the book of Job was an angel of the heavenly court who served as a tester of Job's virtue and good intentions. In the text of 1 Chronicles 21:1-8, Satan's "testing" role has become one of alluring David to sin. There is, then, a gradual transition from the idea of one who is an emissary of Yahweh to one who is pitted against him and his people. It is this latter notion which characterizes the New Testament understanding of Satan or the devil. By the time the book of Wisdom was composed, the devil had been identified with the serpent of the fall in Genesis (Ws 2:24), an identification upheld also in the New Testament (Rv 12:9; 20:2; Jn 8:44; 1 Jn 3:8). The development in demonology comes to the New Testament both from the Old Testament and from extra-biblical Jewish sources of the inter-testamental period, the latter speaking of angels that fall from God's favor and become man's moral opponents. Satan is eventually relegated to their ranks and becomes the chief representative of evil's domain. In the New Testament, he is spoken of as a fallen angel (Lk 10:18; 1 P 2:41; Jude 6) and, as the great adversary of God, he must be overcome in the eschatological conflict. In short he is the concrete expression of that age-old evil which Christ had come to vanquish.

In the Gospels Satan is confronted and overthrown on his own terrain, that of the debilitated and deformed human condition, where, since his primordial appearance in the garden of Genesis, he has been wreaking havoc. He first had to be contended with in the ugliness of blindness, lameness, personal possession of human beings and physical death itself as a prelude to his final overthrowal in the death and resurrection of Christ. This is not to exclude the conflict with Satan on the level of human sinfulness itself which, as we shall see, certainly receives ample play in the Gospels; but it is to see this former type of conflict as its necessary complement.

Since evil finds its first expression in the sinful action of men which, in turn, reaps its fruit in the physical order, the Gospels repeatedly posit the connection between personal sin and sickness. In fact, there are moments where the correlation between the two is clearly specified. The healing of the paralytic (Mk 2:1-12; Mt 9:1-8; Lk 5:17-26) is a case in point. Taking the Marcan account, the most primitive of the three, we note an interesting combination of features. After underscoring the industry of the four men in getting the paralytic before Jesus with the obvious hope of a cure, the narrative in verse 5 takes an unexpected turn. In no way directly addressing himself to the man's illness, Jesus assures him: "My son, your sins are forgiven." A discussion on the power to forgive sin continues between Jesus and his Jewish opponents (not the paralytic, his friends, or the assembled crowd). Only in verse 11b does Jesus return to the point at issue, restoring the man to health to the amazement and edification of the assembled crowd. The abrupt insertion of the forgiveness-of-sins topic, in addition to indications of "stitching" in the rather uneven flow of the Greek text in Mark (upon whom Matthew and Luke at a later date are dependent), has led some critics to conclude that two distinct episodes from Jesus' ministry—one concerning the healing, the other, the power of sin remission—have been joined in the early tradition of the Church's teaching. Whether this did occur or the episode actually transpired as it is narrated in the Synoptics, the point of the narrative is the same. Jesus clearly comes with the power to forgive sin, seen in the eyes of his Jewish contemporaries as an arrogant and blasphemous arrogation of divine author- ity. Jesus does not back away from his claim but vindi- cates it by extending the same power to the healing of sin's victim, the broken body of the paralytic man. The conclusion is that he who comes as God's unique emis- sary has a power over evil which extends to both sin and sickness; its exercise over the latter is more evident and in less need of proof, but its extension to the former is more difficult and more central to the mission of Christ.

The pericope is an apt illustration of our thesis. It should be noted that it is nowhere stated that the man is paying the price of his sins, nor is there any of the quid- pro-quo thinking that has been encountered in the Old Testament. The man is a sinner in the sense that all men are sinners; the circumstances of his cure provide the opportunity to point up Christ's authority over two lev- els of Satan's influence. As we have noted, there is even question as to whether the two topics of the narrative were part of the original encounter. But what is impor- tant and much to the point is the recognition that both Jesus himself and the early Church were heir to the long-established belief that the evils of suffering and sin are inherently related. The belief that Jesus came to deal with both is the point of the story.

Against this background of eschatological invasion in the dethronement of Satan the miracles of the synoptic Gospels should be read. It is, of course, particularly noticeable in cases of diabolical possession where the confrontation is direct. In episodes like that of the man with the unclean spirit in Mk 1:21-27, the seemingly unbridgeable chasm that separates the forces of evil and good is spanned by Christ as he evicts the evil spirit from its domain. To the spirit's query: "What do we have in common with you, Jesus of Nazareth?", the response is strong and imperious: "Be muzzled and come out of him" (1:24-25). The End Time battle is underway in the ministry of Jesus and the Gospels leave no doubt as to who will be the ultimate victor. It is quite likely that at least some of the cases of diabolical possession instanced in the synoptics would be classified differently by modern medicine and psychiatry. It is undeniable that a case such as that of the "possessed" boy (Mk 9:14-29) bears evident symptoms of epilepsy. But in biblical research we are dealing with limits imposed by the thought patterns and cultural outlook of the time of composition. Latter-day Judaism and first-century Christianity, and in this there seems to be no reason to exclude Jesus himself, lacked the benefits of later knowledge in this and many other areas; what was not lacking was the realization that moral evil permeated many sectors of human existence, taking its toll in the total complex of human life. Sickness was a **mastix** or scourge (Mk 3:10; 5:29, 34), a constant reminder of man's sinfulness as well as the inherent limits of his earthly lot.

The same notion of confrontation emerges in the story of the stilling of the storm, especially as it appears in Mark (4:35-41). Again, the fact that modern man does not identify a turbulent sea with the presence of personified evil forces or mythological sea monsters, does not rob the episode of its theological point. Christ has come to do battle with evil and the tempest is another case in point. He addresses the sea in personal terms, strongly akin to those of the possessed man in Mk 1:21-27. The wind is "rebuked" and the sea ordered "to be silent" and "muzzled" (4:39), with the latter expressions lacking in the less primitive Matthew and Luke.

Nowhere is this power of Jesus more striking than when he opposed death itself. The Old Testament converges in seeing death as evil's greatest stronghold. It represents the definitive and irrevocable separation from God and the realm of life; only in the later pages of the Old Testament is there clear recognition of Yahweh's wresting power in effecting the resurrection of the dead. In the synoptics, the Lucan account of the bereft widow's son (7:11-17) and the account of Jairus' daughter (Mk 5:21-43; Mt 9:18-26; Lk 8:40-56) present an especially strong intervention of **dynamis** or divine power. They are Messianic signs in a twofold sense, as representing Christ's conflict against Satan and as symbolizing the restoration from spiritual death to life which Christ effects in the life of every believer. Such activity evokes recognition that the final age has dawned, seen in the reaction of the crowd to the restoration of the widow's son: "God has **visited** his people" (Lk 7:16), an Old Testament expression often connected with eschatological expectations. Such episodes are at the same time a prelude to the ultimate triumph over the forces of evil to be realized in Christ's own victory over the grave.

Old Testament thinking on retribution, therefore, has deeply influenced the miracle stories. One cannot gainsay the presence of other didactic features as well; the importance of faith, for example, cuts deeply into the miracle story genre. But they are principally signs of the final era, actualized in the presence of God's emissary, drawing heavily on the relationship between sin and suffering. This is the significance of the reply of Jesus to the disciples of the Baptist when he is asked if he be the Messiah. The answer is indirect but clearly Messianic in its allusion to the eschatology of Isaiah 35:5f.: "Go and report to John what you have seen and heard. The blind recover their sight, cripples walk, lepers are cured, the deaf hear, dead men are raised to life, and the poor have the good news preached to them" (Lk 7:22).

It is more difficult to speak of the miracles in John's

Gospel in this vein. The emphasis does not fall on them as signs of the Kingdom's inauguration in the overthrowal of Satan. They are "signs" (semeia) of another type, reflecting on the sensible level a deeper spiritual reality. Thus the story of providing the wedding guests with wine at Cana (2:1-10) is symbolic of the abundance of spiritual riches (drawing on Old Testament imagery) attendant upon the Kingdom's coming. The blind man (ch. 9) represents the state of spiritual blindness from which man can be wrested only in the full acceptance of Jesus as Lord and Son of God. The account of Lazarus' restoration to life (ch. 11) is one of the most striking miracles of Jesus' ministry, triggering, in John's Gospel, the decisive steps of his enemies to eliminate Jesus once and for all (11:45ff.). The evidently important character of this miracle makes the complete silence of the synoptics on the event addedly problematic. Yet, that which was implicit in such narratives in the synoptics becomes foremost in John, as a sign of that transformation or "resurrection" which takes place in the believer when he comes to faith, an event in the Christian life which is in itself a presage of resurrection on the last day. On the other hand, the explicit synoptic idea of the defeat of Satan is, at least, implicit in John, where the miracles are also referred to as "works" (erga), connoting a continuation in Jesus of the mighty "works" of Yahweh in the Old Testament. In creation, the liberation from Egypt, and the taking of the promised land, Yahweh was at work in triumphing over evil. In this regard the ministry of Jesus is a prolongation of the divine activity.

This theme of liberation in the action of Jesus is clearly seen in the Johannine narrative of the cure of the blind man (ch. 9) where the main emphasis of the narrative falls on Jesus' power to effect a transition from **spiritual** blindness to sight. But the entire theme evolves within the scenario of the **physical** cure of a blind man.

The implications of the disciples' opening question are by now all too familiar: "Rabbi, was it his sin or that of his parents that caused him to be born blind?" (9:2). The traditional theory of retribution met obvious difficulties in the case of the child defective from birth—its most cogent explanation lay in relating the defect to the sin of the child's progenitors (Cf. Ex 20:5). Jesus in the Johannine narrative moves away from such a line of argumentation and once again divorces himself from this direct cause-and-effect type of reasoning. He deals only with the purpose of the illness in God's plan. "It was no sin either of this man or his parents. Rather, it was to let God's works (erga) show forth in him" (9:3). The meaning of Jesus' response is illustrated in the chapter as a whole. There is no doubt that the blind man's plight remains a mystery; there is no attempt on Jesus' part to explain it, other than by excluding a commonly accepted explanation. But the blindness does serve a purpose. It affords the opportunity for God's creative "work" to be manifested, a "work" which includes liberating the man from the darkness of physical blindness; but, even more importantly, it becomes a symbol of that transfer from the darkness of sin to the light of faith, which only the Son of God is able to realize. This is the "work" of liberation shared by the Father and the Son.

In underscoring this as the "work" of God, which implies divine power and might and is ultimately directed to manifestation of his glory, we are viewing the eschatological conflict of the synoptics in different terms and with more theological subtlety. In overcoming the man's blindness, on both levels, Jesus is victorious over the realm of darkness. But there is specific attention given in John to the man's suffering in itself. It serves as an important vehicle for the manifestation of God's design. In the same way it was essential Lazarus die before Jesus reached Bethany that, through his restoration to life, "the Son of God may be glorified" (11:4). Without being extensive in its elaboration, the Fourth Gospel throws a new light on the question. It is an idea that is developed more fully in Paul. Questions on the precise "why" of suffering are doomed to failure. To see it as part of the adversary's camp is valid and rests on a firm biblical basis. But suffering and death are not completely negative. They have been woven into the very texture of salvation, as the climax of Jesus' life amply illustrates. It is the medium through which God works to manifest his glory. This was the lesson of suffering that Jesus himself had to learn, as the author of Hebrews states (5:7), a lesson that cannot be lost on his followers.

Jesus, The Servant of the Lord

It happened that an Ethiopian eunuch, a court official in charge of the entire treasury of Candace . . . of the Ethiopians, had come on a pilgrimage and was returning home. He was sitting in the carriage reading the prophet Isaiah. The Spirit said to Philip, "Go and catch up with that carriage." Philip ran ahead and heard the man reading the prophet Isaiah. He said to him: "Do you really grasp what you are reading?" "How can I," the man replied, "unless someone explains it to me?". . . This was the passage of Scripture he was reading:

Like a sheep he was led to the slaughter,
like a lamb before its shearer he was silent
and opened not his mouth.
In his humiliation he was deprived of justice.
Who will ever speak of his posterity,
for he is deprived of his life on earth?

The eunuch said to Philip, "Tell me, if you will,

of whom the prophet says this—himself or
someone else?" Philip started out with this
Scripture passage as his starting point, telling
him the good news of Jesus (Ac 8:27-35).

In the person of Jesus the many-faceted problem of
human suffering and death reaches a focal point and
takes on a new meaning. To see the inherent relationship
between sin and suffering, even while keeping the connection broad, is to conclude that we suffer because we
share in man's initial rebellion both through inheritance
and personal ratification. But to say this alone is to deprive Christian suffering of its positive content. To de-
termine its value in a Christian context, we must first
examine its meaning in the life of Christ himself as this
is grasped and expressed in the New Testament.

The account of the meeting between Philip and the
eunuch cited above is an instance of early Christianity's
propensity to see Jesus as the Servant of Yahweh. The
eunuch is reading from the fourth Servant song, whose
central figure he cannot identify; the passage serves as
a starting point for Philip's catechesis. The identification
of Jesus with the Servant seems to have been relatively
early in the Church and appears with a remarkable de-
gree of frequency either explicitly or by insinuation.
Why is this the case? It may have been derived from
Jesus himself who, gradually realizing the distinctive
and paradoxical character of his Messianic mission, saw
the correspondence between his mission and that of the
Isaian figure. In avoiding the overtones of a political
Messiah, Jesus may have settled on the Servant as an
End-Time personality devoid of any nationalistic conno-
tations. But about this we can only conjecture. An argument of **"decuit, potuit, fecit"** is not too convincing to the
critical eye of the historian and the strong catechetical
imprint of the Church on the New Testament makes

affirmations of certitude very difficult. At most it can reasonably be argued that a title with such extensive coinage at an early stage may well have derived from Christ himself.

We are on surer ground when we address ourselves to the Church's use of the Servant image. There is no question that the Church found the theme theologically suitable in describing Christ's salvific work. The reason for this becomes clear when we consider that a variety of Old Testament titles—Messiah, Prophet, Son of Man— fell rather naturally into place once, through Easter faith, the lordship of Christ was recognized. He was not simply a literal fulfillment of the hopes registered by these titles. But, in going beyond them, he had subsumed them and therefore, **mutatis mutandis,** they could readily be applied to him. But what of his suffering? Could this aspect be given any possible Old Testament justification? It was at this point that the Servant songs came to the fore; notwithstanding the mystery surrounding them they do depict eschatological deliverance through the medium of suffering. Thus, the theme of the Servant of the Lord, coupled with the more traditional Messianic titles, gave a strong Scriptural base to Jewish Christianity's claim.

The point is well illustrated in one of Peter's early addresses (Ac 3:12-26). Before his fellow Israelites, he gives post-Pentecostal witness to the belief that Christ represents the fulfillment of Old Testament aspirations. He is proclaimed as Messiah (vv. 18, 20), the Prophet (vv. 22f.), the Holy and Just One (v. 14), the Author of Life (v. 15), the One in whose name healing is effected (v. 16); but at the same time he is the Servant, handed over and disowned (v. 13), yet now raised up as the source of blessing and conversion (v. 26). The conclusion may strike us as Christian overstatement: "God has brought to fulfillment by this means what he announced

long ago through all the prophets: that his Messiah would
suffer" (3:18). It would take more than a little good will
to accept the idea of a suffering Messiah as even a partial
element of Old Testament prophetism, not to speak of
"all the prophets." The exaggerated emphasis is Luke's,
drawing on an early Christian tradition of the suffering
Messiah which, in light of the fact that the Messiah **did**
suffer, read many parts of the Old Testament, especially
the psalms of the suffering just man, as part of prophetic
insight. But it was the Songs of the Servant that served
as an important point of departure in the early Church's
understanding of the suffering Messiah.

What were seen as the main points of likeness between Christ and the Servant? There was, first of all,
the vicarious suffering and death, the offering of life in
humble resignation in the interests of others. In addition,
both figures are represented as mediators of a new covenant which embraces Jew and Gentile alike. That Jesus
establishes the new alliance, spoken of most clearly in
Jeremiah 31:31ff., is a central New Testament theme; it
is also at the heart of the Servant's mission. And, finally,
there is God's ultimate vindication of his Servant. As
was noted earlier, this is left rather general and unspecified in the fourth Servant song; in the New Testament it
is identified with the resurrection and glorification of
Christ. Critics discuss which of these elements was initially more dominant. In the Petrine speech already cited,
there is reference to both the Servant Jesus' betrayal
and consignment to death as well as his being "raised
up." In the Eucharistic liturgical formula of the synoptics' last supper narrative, the Servant as covenant-
mediator comes strongly to the fore. In any event, the
identification is clearly established and, apart from Acts,
is woven at different points into the Gospels in the
course of their composition. It is a theme which has less
importance for Paul.

Once firmly established, the Servant theme served another important function, more apologetic in character. In situating Jesus clearly in a prophetic Old Testament framework, it explained the enigma of his inglorious death to Jew and Gentile alike. What he endured through the evil machinations of men represented no triumph on their part; the Son of God could not be victimized by mortals. As difficult as it might be to understand, that which had occurred was an integral part of God's salvific plan. Thus the Lucan Jesus can counter the distress of the Emmaus disciples, distraught over the seeming failure of the one in whom they had hoped, with the question: "Did not the Messiah have to suffer these things and enter into his glory?" (Lk 24:26), as he then illustrates his point from Moses and the prophets. Christ had suffered because the Father had so decreed. While this presents theological problems of its own, with which the New Testament is forced to come to grips, it has at the same time placed the suffering and death of Jesus on a different plane, the full implications of which will only slowly emerge. In taking up death God has done battle with Satan not only on the latter's own terrain but with the use of his opponent's principal weapon as well. The end of life which had long been identified with the realm of sin now passes in a very positive way to the realm of grace. In fact, it has become the principal instrument of man's salvation.

Restricting ourselves principally to the synoptic Gospels, we can see that this idea of the death of Jesus as divinely willed, illustrated in the Servant leitmotif, is strongly fixed in the tradition. In the three synoptics, immediately after the high point of Peter's profession of faith, Jesus speaks of his impending passion (Mk 8: 31ff; Mt 16:21ff; Lk 9:22). It is a "suffering many things" which must be undergone and which is described in detail: rejection, death, resurrection on the third day.

It is extremely unlikely that the historical Jesus spoke of his imminent trial in such precise terms, but the fact that it has been specified and elaborated **post eventum** only underscores the extent to which primitive Christianity saw all these particulars as divinely willed and salvific. It is the fourth Servant song which serves as the principal basis for the belief in the necessity of all that will transpire; the three elements of suffer, consign to death and rise, all find an echo in Isaiah 53. In addition, three times in the fourth Song the Servant is said to be "handed over" to death by God, with the same verb used by the synoptics in later predictions of the passion (cf. Mk 10:33, Mt 20:18; Lk 18:32).

In both the theophanies of Jesus' baptism and his transfiguration, the Father's designation of his Son is based in part on his being identified with the Servant. Thus he is referred to as "the beloved" at the baptism in all the synoptics which, combined with the royal messianism present in the added "my Son" references, succinctly summarizes Jesus' role as Servant-Messiah. The same designation appears in the transfiguration, with Luke (9:35) substituting the equally strong Servant reference, "my chosen one." The fourth Gospel's parallel to the synoptics' baptism scene presents Jesus as the lamb of God (1:29), which may be seen against the background of the Servant described as the lamb led to the slaughter in Isaiah 53.

This use of the Isaian Servant, whether explicitly or by allusion, serves to point up the divinely preordained sufferings of Christ as an integral part of Old Testament prophecy. As such it goes beyond any idea of mere passive acceptance. If the death of Jesus is compared to the grain of wheat which must die in order to bear fruit (Jn 12:24), then that death must be seen as necessary and directly related to the resurrection and its fruits. It is deeply woven into the fabric of salvation. But if we were to stop there, we would revert to a type of theology in which the offended Creator exacts his "pound of flesh" from his rebellious creatures through the execution of the divinely commissioned representative of a sinful humanity.

Christian soteriology lies on a much deeper level. It is above all a matter of love expressed in obedience. Only when all that is summed up in the **pathemata** or sufferings of Christ is related to the love which underlies them can it redound to the benefit of "the many." The heart of the matter lies in Christ's willing submission to the awesome power of death as the most perfect expression of his love for the Father and for his fellow man. He did not face suffering and death with a cold and detached stoicism nor with some sort of prophetic insight that told him his third day resurrection was inevitable. Every fibre of his being shrank from what lay before him.

This is the only meaning that can be conferred on the Gethsemane narrative, and any attempts to rationalize it do so at the risk of robbing Christian soteriology of one of its most important features. What is important is that notwithstanding his sense of revulsion Christ did not turn back. God wanted to reconcile man to himself and in a way that would irrevocably recall the horror of sin and the power of love. Christ shared these sentiments, he walked the lonely and awesome path that has made us one with God. How else were we to know what the love of God meant? It is one thing for John to define God as love; it is only when the fourth Gospel shows us how that love was actualized that its import is realized.

In underscoring the integration of death into the salvific plan, it would be wrong to conclude that God is pleased with death or suffering. The offering of death to the God of life is anomalous at best. God and death are at opposite poles, a fact which any soteriological theory cannot escape. This is most evident in recent studies on Old Testament sacrifice which are at pains to show how victim immolation can be fitted into Yahwistic cult.[2] The death or destruction of the offering was necessary as the only means by which it could be "transferred" to the realm of the divine and at the same time deprive man of its benefits. In the case of animal offerings, for instance, the essential priestly action is seen in the sprinkling of the blood, connected with life, not in the slaughter of the victim which was ordinarily left to others. Although the killing was necessary, the sacerdotal function is related to the element of life. Hence, it is with the aspect of self-deprivation and communion with God made possible by the immolation, rather than with death itself, that Israelite sacrifice is concerned. It is in life that God glories, a truth that is accentuated in the case of his own Son.

Hence, the Father does not look with satisfaction on the death of Jesus but he does respond to the sentiment of total self-donation which underlies the death. It is this posture of love and commitment that gives suffering a new dimension in the New Testament; it is this which wrenches death from the realm of evil and sets it firmly on the side of good. Man is forever reconciled when the new Adam reverses the resounding "I will not" of the first Adam by his firm and submissive "I will," even to the extent of dying. In the face of all the contradictory strains on the human conscience that urge him toward betrayal, man is forever challenged by that single life which tells him, in very concrete terms, the extent to which Love was willing to go to make him free.

It has been often noted that the New Testament has no philosophy of death, no ultimately satisfying explana-

---

(2) Cf., e.g., De Vaux, R., **Ancient Israel,** London, Dartman, Longman, Todd, 1961, ch. 13, "The Religious Significance of Sacrifice."

tion. Although its terms were different, death confronted Christ as it confronts everyone. He accepted it as a fact. In so doing, he further strengthens the bonds that link him with all of us. It is this point of identity with a suffering God that has sustained many a Christian faced with the trial of his own lot. At the same time, it should be affirmed that there is no Christian mystique of suffering for its own sake. There is no indication that Christ relished it or asked for it; what he did do was accept it. The New Testament does not ask the Christian to pray for suffering or pain. Authentic Christian asceticism bids us to accept and sanctify our lot and, when the interests of love may demand it, not to avoid the path that may carry us through personal agony. The moment of trial is never detached from that which shapes it and gives it value—the will attuned to God.

The whole question is well summarized in a succinct passage from the Epistle to the Hebrews, whose unknown author has bequeathed us some of the New Testament's greatest theological riches. In the tenth chapter, he compares the sacrifice of Christ with those of the earlier Law, indicating that the former now abrogates the latter. This he does by drawing on Psalm 40 in its Greek translation of the Sepuagint and making it applicable, with a certain amount of exegetical liberty, to the case in point. The psalm in its original context points up the superiority of internal dispositions of obedience over ritual formalism. The author quotes the psalm:

> Sacrifice and offering you did not desire
> but a body you have prepared for me;
> Holocausts and sin offerings you took no
> delight in. Then I said, 'As is written of me
> in the book, I have come to do your will,
> O God' (10:5ff.).

Then he offers his comment:

> First he says, 'Sacrifices and offerings, holo-
> causts and sin offerings,
> you neither desired nor delighted in.'
> (These are offered according to the prescriptions
> of the law). Then he says:
> 'I have come to do your will.'
> In other words, he takes away the first covenant
> to establish the second.
> By this "will," we have been sanctified through
> the offering of the body of Jesus Christ once
> and for all (10:9f).

It can be added that it is the same "will" which directs the mission of the Servant of the Lord in Isaiah and, in turn, has been actualized in the Servant Jesus. As Hebrews further notes, Christ grew in obedience as he suffered, offering "prayers and supplications with loud cries and tears to God" (5:7). A devotional or artistic piety which exaggeratedly emphasizes the physical suffering of Jesus, sometimes to the point of the grotesque, is misdirected, even if well-intentioned. Such stands in sharp contrast with the circumspect and restrained statements of the Gospel passion narratives. We have simply no way of measuring those sufferings and dramatic comparisons are ill-advised. What emerges with unmistakable clarity in the New Testament picture of the Servant Jesus is a total engagement in the will of God. And it is this spirit which must be found in his followers. In fact, the first epistle of Peter takes up the Servant theme in a distinctly exhortatory context as he urges fortitude in the face of suffering.

> It was for this you were called, since Christ
> suffered for you in just this way and left you an
> example, to have you follow in his footsteps.

He did no wrong; no deceit was found in his mouth. When he was insulted, he returned no insult. When he was made to suffer, he did not counter with threats. Instead, he delivered himself up to the One who judges justly. In his own body he brought your sins to the cross, so that all of us, dead to sin, could live in accord with God's will. By his wounds you were healed. At one time you were straying like sheep, but now you have returned to the Shepherd, the Guardian of your souls (2:21-25).

It was the summons of obedience that lay at the heart of Jesus' call, and the call of every Christian since. In responding, one embarks on the troubled waters of pain and suffering. It was not easy then, and it is not easy now. But there is no denying the fact that it is a response which lies within the grasp of all of us.

VI.

LIFE IN DEATH

We are afflicted in every way possible, but we
are not crushed; full of doubts, we never despair.
We are persecuted but never abandoned, we are
struck down but never destroyed. Continually
we carry about in our bodies the dying of Jesus,
so that in our bodies the life of Jesus may also
be revealed. While we live we are constantly
being delivered to death for Jesus' sake, so that
the life of Jesus may be revealed in our mortal
flesh (2 Cor 4:8-11).

Considerations of the problem of evil in the epistles
of Paul antedate, from one point of view, those of the
Gospels. The major part of Paul's literary work dates
from the period between 50 and 60 A.D., whereas the
composition of the earliest Gospel, that of Mark, is generally dated about 65. However, a proper understanding
of the Gospels sees them as a **terminus ad quem** rather
than as a starting point. As a living tradition, transmitted first in oral and then written form, the Gospels
had an extended prior history before being given their
definitive form. Paul was familiar with the catechesis
centering on the life and teaching of Jesus even though
the Gospel material plays no significant role in his writings. He has drawn on this tradition and given expression
to its implications for the Christian life in his letters.
In view of the new and important directions in which he

carries the question of sin and its consequences, we can treat his teaching at this point without doing violence to an accepted historical chronology.

Paul is treated here for another reason. One of his main concerns is relating the suffering and death of Christ to the life of the Christian, the prolongation of the death, as well as the resurrection of the Lord in his followers. The Servant theme, for example, receives scant attention in Paul as a title for Jesus. There is a possible reference to the Servant in the celebrated hymn of Philippians (2:6-11), where the pre-existent Christ makes his descent among men in the "form of a slave," but here Paul would be drawing on the early Christian liturgy as a source, accepting the expression as it stood. Whatever "servant" allusions are present in Paul center more around himself and the trials of the apostolic ministry (Gal 1:15; 2 Cor 4-6), which would be in keeping with his emphasis on the continuation of the mission of Christ in his disciples.

Any treatment of this subject in Paul finds Romans its pivotal point. Sin is an all-pervasive reality, embracing Gentile and Jew alike (Rm 3:9). The evil of their lives is evidence that the Gentiles have never recognized God, even with the partial knowledge they could have derived from creation itself. The Jews are even more culpable; privileged with the revealed law, they have succeeded only in disregarding it.

If it should seem that Paul gives a disproportionate amount of consideration to sin and its consequences, two factors should be borne in mind. First, the power and pervasiveness of sin serves to highlight the victory of Christ, who alone eradicates it at its roots and in its widespread ramifications. In addition, the recognition of sin as it touches the life of the individual is essential for salvation in Pauline thought. Its recognition rules out any notion of self-sufficiency, the greatest obstacle

that man can place to God's saving action. If he underscores sin's force it is to make man conscious of his
radical insufficiency before it and thus wholly dependent
on the power of God, verifying his dictum that in man's
weakness is God's strength.

In the drama of salvation (Rm 5-7), Sin and Death are
personified; together with Adam, the Law, and Christ,
they are the **dramatis personae** of the redemptive epic.
It is through Adam that Sin and Death make their appearance and quickly spread to all mankind. Paul affirms
that sin was a reality even before the promulgation of
the Law even though men did not violate positive pro-
hibitions as Adam did. This he can affirm because there
was never a period when death was not present. Thus
Paul reasserts the long-standing tradition of the relation
between sin and death. In the same line, the death of
which Paul speaks is total, spiritual and physical; it is
the definitive separation from God which is sealed by
bodily death. This is clear from death's parallel with the
life that is brought in Christ; it is spiritual death and
spiritual life that form the antitheses of the parallelism.
The appearance of the Law on this world stage did not
help the cause of good; because of man's inability to
observe it, it only enabled him to specify his wrongdoing with greater accuracy and thus quickly became a
tool of the two other villains of the drama, Sin and Death.

By reason of Adam's rebellion, there is a "state of
sin" which all men inherit and in turn further ratify by
their own acts of wrongdoing. Romans does not speak of
the manner in which this sinful state is transmitted nor
its precise nature—questions which have vexed theo-
logians for centuries. What is clear is that personal sin
alone does not satisfy the requirements for Sin in Romans, Chapter 5 (although it certainly enters in 5:12).
There is a sinful presence which goes beyond its personal ratification in the life of the individual. This seems

to be the whole sense of the parallelism between Adam and Christ. Death (and sin) have come to all men from One, just as grace and life have come from One (cf. 5:15). To put it briefly, personal sin verifies the presence of Sin. It is this state of affairs that evokes the "wrath of God," the inevitable judgment demanded by the existence of Sin which is to be meted out in the final days or in the course of history by acts of divine chastisement. It is man himself, not God, who is the principal cause inasmuch as he rejects the ever-present love of the Creator and thereby condemns himself.

Despite the dismal picture presented by Sin's reign, it is as nothing in comparison with the gift that has come in Christ. The reconciliation achieved in the new Adam outstrips in every way the chaos inherited from the first Adam. The latter brought condemnation, death and the proliferation of sin through disobedience; the former brings acquittal, life, and the superabundance of grace through obedience. In the drama's climax, Sin, Law and Death are rendered powerless by the victory of the new Adam.

Yet Paul elsewhere states: "You have been bought at a great price!" (1 Cor 7:23). How did God wrest man from the power of evil in Paul's thought? How was reconciliation attained? It is not simply a question of a juridical acquittal or moral absolution but rather, once again, it involved entering the strong man's house in order to disarm him, doing battle with Goliath on his own terrain. While in no way a sinner himself, Christ assumes all Sin's consequences. He appears in a weak, sufferable flesh that has been victimized by sin. Suffering in that flesh he definitively evicts its proprietor; sin is put to death in sinful flesh. Strikingly akin to the sacrifices of the levitical law, the flesh of Christ becomes an offering for sin. "Then God sent his Son in the likeness of sinful flesh as a sin offering, thereby condemning sin in the flesh" (Rm 8:3; 2 Cor 5:21). It is a forceful teaching which must be taken at face value. Modern social and human concern places great emphasis on "experiencing," "identifying with," and "personal empathy," expressions which fall short as surrogates for Christian redemption.

The age-old battle between man and evil had left man the loser, with no gains, only losses. The Victor had taken his toll; a weakened flesh, human travail, and the prospect of final death represented the price that had been paid. Man had been shackled by his own wrong-doing. It is a story that stems from the first chapters of Genesis, only to repeat itself on page after page of the Old Testament. It is God himself who bridges the chasm of irreconcilable opposites by assuming flesh himself and freely appropriating the damages of man's undoing. While he did not know sin, the whole problem of evil came to rest in his person. Through the generosity of personal self-donation, the pre-existent Son came to know physical deprivation, the suffering of the body, and the even greater pain of rejection and ingratitude. He faced death with a deeply human plea for deliverance and breathed his last praying the psalm of a desolate man who felt abandoned even by God. This is the reality that has set us free, that has broken the shackles once and for all. It was a battle clearly fought in the enemy camp; Christ made his own the consequences of sin in the fullest sense of the word. This Pauline realism cannot be diluted. A Christology which attempts to uphold the divinity of Christ by blunting the vital cutting edge of his total humanity does an injustice to New Testament soteriology. If the Scriptures assert that he was like us in everything except sin, then the full consequences of that statement have to be accepted. To paraphrase the Philippians hymn, Christ redeemed us not by jealously guarding divine equality, but by a profound self-emptying which made him both man and servant. It was by dying in that carnal body that the body of glory was born. It is the risen body of Christ that becomes a vivifying Spirit, transforming mortal flesh from that point on. It is for this reason that the death and resurrection are inseparable in Paul as the cause and source of man's salvation.

We have previously spoken of the underlying sentiments of obedience and love that give meaning to redemption. The same theme repeats itself in Paul. Christ is not a scapegoat to appease divine justice. Disobedience was at the root of the first Adam's rebellion; obedience is its remedy in the mission of the new Adam, according to the parallelism of Romans (5:19). Yet, it was an obedience that corresponded to a love on God's part which had never been lacking despite man's refusal to respond. If Paul gives so much attention to the death of Christ, it is because it embodies the act of love. It is thinkable, says the Apostle, that one might give his life for a just man; what is unthinkable is one's surrender of life for the guilty or, as in the case of the sinner, one who had constituted himself an enemy. "It is precisely in this that God proves his love for us: that while we were still sinners, Christ died for us" (Rm 5:7f). It is the impact that this love has upon the Christian that gives him his firmest hope. It is so unspeakable that it dwarfs to insignificance every human trial or conflict. In the lyric climax to Romans 8, Paul envisions no earthly hardship (trial, persecution, hunger, the sword) or ultraterrestrial power (death, heavenly beings, astrological forces) which is capable "of separating us from the love of God that comes to us in Christ Jesus our Lord" (Rm 8:35-39).

But Paul does not stop there. His pastoral concerns lead him to stress the meaning of this teaching in the life of the individual Christian. The salvific act of death-resurrection is to be appropriated and prolonged in Christ's followers. The first response is faith, an acceptance of and adherence to the person of Christ, which recognizes the implications of death-resurrection. The underlying sentiments of Christ are continued in the Christian, as Paul speaks of the "obedience of faith" (Rm 1:5, 16:26). The initiative in applying the fruits of redemption is always God's; it is a good that man must recognize he is totally incapable of realizing by any effort of his own. Yet, a response is demanded—that of faith. This must be a full and unqualified commitment, dynamic rather than static, which is destined to effect an ever-deeper union with the One to whom it is directed. Paul states that it is so all-pervasive that it envelops his whole existence: ". . . the life I live now is not my own; Christ is living in me. I still live my human life, but it is a life of faith in the Son of God who loved me and gave himself for me" (Gal 2:20). It results in a confidence in the fidelity of the Lord to his promises; it is active with an activity which involves man but, even more importantly, God himself. As part of the whole economy of salvation, it remains always a gift.

For Paul, Baptism is the necessary concomitant of faith, its sacramental expression. In Baptism, the Christian is incorporated into Christ, personally and ontologically; it is Paul who explains the basic meaning of this new incorporation. The Christian enters into the death-resurrection of Christ, and the death-resurrection is prolonged in the life of the Christian. It does not suffice to say that the Christian is born again unto a new life, which certainly identifies him with the risen Lord. But the Christian also dies—to sin, to self, to the Law; the crucifixion becomes real in his own life. "I have been crucified with Christ . . ." (Gal 2:19). Thus, the Christian is transfixed in death in appropriating the passion of the Lord. In fact, for Paul this is the only death that really matters; it is a death that is productive of life, a life which is interminable, the full fruits of which will be evident with personal resurrection. Once one has passed

through the portals of baptismal death, he has no further
death to experience, spiritual death being excluded by
the commitment, physical death, being nothing more
than transitional. Only perseverance is called for. The
End Time, with its resplendent immortality, will verify
the Scriptures: "Death is swallowed up in victory. O
death, where is your victory? O death, where is your
sting? The sting of death is sin, and sin gets its power
from the law. But thanks be to God who has given us
the victory through our Lord Jesus Christ. Be steadfast
and persevering, my brothers" (1 Cor 15:54-58).

In an imagery which may reflect the early Christian's
descent into the baptismal pool, we read in Romans:
"How can we who died to sin go on living in it? Are you
not aware that we who were baptized into Christ Jesus
were baptized into his death? Through baptism in his
death we were buried with him, so that, just as Christ
was raised from the dead by the glory of the Father, we,
too, might live a new life" (6:2ff.). Thus, the victory
which Christ attained by putting sin to death in his own
flesh must be actualized in the life of his disciples. By
reason of its permanent and transcendent character,
that salvific act realized at a determined period in space
and time now goes beyond those limitations. Christ now
lives, having incorporated into his present existence the
experience of his suffering and death. He is the glorified
Lamb of the book of Revelation who is at the same time
recognized as the Lamb who had been slain (Rv 5:6).
The Christian cannot adhere to Christ without appropriating the same experience. This is not mere figurative language, any more than the sacraments are mere
symbols. The sacraments bring to bear in the concrete
the saving action of Christ, and the sacrament of Baptism
reproduces in the recipient the death and rising of
Christ. The new life in Christ, which implies assuming
the dispositions which were his (described by Paul as

the donning of a new garment), also brings about a death to sin in all its forms. This means a burial of the "old man," a separation from the realm of death in all its forms which, for Paul, is total and irrevocable.

Can it be said then that the eschatological battle is over? Does not our daily experience belie such categorical affirmations? In one sense the work is completed, sin has been vanquished, what has been accomplished in Christ will never and need never be repeated. On the other hand, the final fruits of that victory are not yet ours and will not be until Christ realizes completely his salvific mission and hands the Kingdom back to the Father (1 Cor 15:24).

There remains in Paul that tension between the "already" and the "not yet," between an eschatology that is realized and yet still future. On the one hand, we have been transferred to the realm of the Spirit, the new life, as members of God's household, his planting, to mention but a few Pauline images. But that which is completed from the point of view of the "wholly other," the transcendent, the divine, is still being realized in space and time, in the historical order. So it is that Paul goes between the two orders, with salvation at one point achieved, at another, not yet achieved. In brief, we have died with Christ and now must live out that dying in the human and temporal conflicts that arise between flesh and spirit, the old man and the new, between death and life. The victory realized in Christ will only be complete when it is realized in his members, and so the struggle must go on. It is clear where the Christian finds himself in this conflict and what is its eventual outcome.

The Christian operates not on mere promises but from a state of being, one in which victory has been achieved. But he also carries a burden, the burden of a death, from which he does not detachedly step aside in baptism but which he incorporates into his very existence. Just as the Lamb in glory is still marked by the wounds of his passion, so too Paul can say: "Continually we carry about in our bodies the dying of Jesus, so that in our bodies the life of Jesus may also be revealed" (2 Cor 4:10).

Sorrow and joy are the lot of everyone. The same was true of Christ himself. We can summarize his sorrows in the one word, "death," and his joys in "resurrection." Yet, that which is the lot of all men is different for the Christian. On the surface his struggles may seem to be the same and in some instances are. But the basic struggle arises from commitment to the Gospel; it is this more than anything else that causes him pain. In having in himself "the mind of the Lord Jesus," the Christian is called to obedience no less than his Master even though it does not take him down the same historical path. It is unwavering fidelity to the will of God that will produce its own measure of suffering and pain. This is the living-out of the baptismal death; it plunges one into the passion of the Lord while, at the same time, it extends that passion to the present moment.

Much is said in our time about tensions. Perhaps the accelerated pace of life has made them more evident, but it is safe to say that no period in history has found them absent. A certain measure of tension is necessary; nothing can be accomplished without it. It is clear that tension is part of the Christian life. With Pentecostal fervor we praise the Lord for the gift of the Spirit, but the presence of the Spirit is not all sweetness and light. The Spirit sets goals that are at complete variance with "this body of death," and both are at work within us. Our course is set, our goal is clear, and the means to reach it are present, yet sin in its death throes is at work within us also. Simply stated: "If you live according to the flesh, you will die; but if by the spirit you put to death the evil deeds of the body, you will live" (Rm 8:13). This is the conflict of the Christian life, the principal cause of its tension. It is a bipolarity that explains what it means to experience the death and resurrection of Christ.

Paul carries his thesis even further in terms of his understanding of what it means to be "in Christ." The realism with which Paul uses this phrase goes beyond a moral affinity between Christ and the Christian, or even ontological influence in terms of the life of grace. The unity between the person of the risen Christ and the baptized is so real and intimate that it constitutes "one body" (1 Cor 10:16-17) and can even be compared to the sexual union in "one flesh" (1 Cor 6:15f.). The identity that it establishes is such that Paul can say: . . . "the life I live now is not my own; Christ is living in me" (Gal 2:20). That which effects this union is the Spirit of the risen Christ, binding the disciple to his Master and as a new-born member of the household of God, enabling him to address his Creator as **Abba,** Father, the same familiar term used by Christ himself. It is this same Spirit that produces the state of death and life in the Christian.

On the basis of this unity, it is asserted that the Christian shares in the suffering and death of Christ. Can it also be said that Christ shares in the suffering of the Christian? For Paul the answer is in the affirmative. The life of the Spirit makes the Head inseparable from the members. The intense reality of this union says more than connatural sentiments or dispositions. The unity is such that Christ experiences and appropriates as his own that which is endured by the disciple, just as the converse is true of the disciple with reference to Christ. It cannot be forgotten that weakness and suffering, so fundamentally expressive of man's radical insufficiency, are the fertile terrain in which the action of God is most evident. What God works in weakness can be clearly seen as his work, with human resources at a minimum. Hence, the New Testament emphasis on the all-important spirit of lowliness, that of the **anawim**, with pride seen as the greatest obstacle to salvation. As a result of baptism, then, the Spirit of Christ active in the trials and afflictions of his incorporated members makes this the work of Christ in an even stronger sense, since Christ is suffering in his members. Thus the great importance attached by Paul to the virtue of endurance, the determined attachment to the will of the Lord in the face of trials (e.g., Rm 5:3f.; 15:4f.; 2 Cor 6:4; 12:12). It is trial that produces endurance which, in turn, is proof that we have stood the test and as such is a pledge of future glory. It is the channel through which the body of Christ is being built up. This is why Paul gives a particular Christological value to tribulations endured in the work of evangelization.

We have noted that it was the love and submissiveness of Jesus, underlying his death, that served as the basis of redemption, finding their sequel in the glory of resurrection. It is this same Spirit of love which now passes to the baptized as Christ continues his redeeming mission. This is what it means "to walk in the Spirit" and it implies a personal crucifixion for each Christian as he is involved in the struggle between flesh and spirit (Rm 8). Hence, the paradox. In the very act of applying the effects of his victory and sharing the fruits of his suffering, Christ continues the experience of his passion. Why? Because the Head is inseparable from the members.

Only when this premise is accepted can we understand much of what Paul teaches. He will use an expression such as "suffer with" **(sympascho)** to express the

inter-relatedness of Christ and the disciple. "But if we
are children, we are heirs as well: heirs of God, heirs of
Christ, if only we suffer with him so as to be glorified
with him. I consider the suffering of the present to be
as nothing compared with the glory to be revealed in us"
(Rm 8:17f.). Patient endurance of trial, with the same
"will" that Jesus manifested, will ultimately lead to the
same glory. In the interim, the "suffering with" involves
the Christian's share in the act of the Lord's death and
Christ's appropriation of the sufferings of his members.
Yet, it is not tribulation without its own consolation; the
Christian is comforted by the presence of the victorious
Spirit, which bears within it the seed of an inalterable
hope, as well as by the lived example of the Master who
went before him. "As we have shared much in the suffering of Christ, so through Christ do we share abundantly
in his consolation" (2 Cor 1:5).

In the light of the foregoing, we are in a better position to understand the enigmatic text of Colossians which
has long been a "crux interpretum." One of the captivity
epistles, Colossians is written during one of Paul's peri-
ods of imprisonment, possibly his final one at Rome. If
the hypothesis be correct, Paul is in an advantageous
position to evaluate his sufferings, both present and past.
Since they are sufferings endured in the interests of the
Gospel they are the cause of rejoicing, as the Apostle
states in the celebrated passage: "Even now I find my
joy in the suffering I endure for you. In my own flesh
I fill up what is lacking in the sufferings of Christ for
the sake of his body, the Church" (1:24). How can anything be lacking in the sufferings of Christ? If the death-
resurrection is a once-for-all event, wrought by God's
own Son, how can it be incomplete? The problem arises
only when the redemption is seen in essentialist or absolute terms, when there is no adequate distinction be-

tween the finality of Christ's passion and victory and its historical application, between the "already" and "not yet" of Pauline thought.

Paul does not view redemption as self-contained, in a state of static completeness, to which mankind is subsequently related. It has an ongoing dynamism viewed in the total historical context. Christ is not simply a model to be imitated; he is active and present in history as Saviour. Seen in this sense, salvation is not complete, nor are the tribulations which accompany it. To say that something is lacking to the sufferings of Christ is not a pious figure of speech. As long as the Spirit of Christ is actualizing the promised total redemption, the passion is continuing. It will continue until the body is completely built up to the "full measure of Christ," with all the apostolic labor and suffering that Christ must endure in his members brought to completion. This is not to deprive the one redemptive act of its inherent efficacy; it is complete in the sense that we shall never be redeemed again.

What God wrought in his Son is unsurpassed and unsurpassable; it is **the** definitive act of reconciliation. But it does not stand by itself; it is essentially related to those for whom it is intended. It is actually being lived out by Christ. This is its historical, existential dimension, which is central to understanding the Colossians text or Pauline soteriology in general. The shift in recent theology to considerations of the future, the influence of the End Time on the present, and the importance of Christian hope for an incomplete Christianity, offers a much needed balance. Ignorant of a central thrust of the New Testament, too much theology had been centered on the past. Too often it was a question of a detailed analysis of the redemptive value of Christ's death (often to the exclusion of the resurrection as salvific), and its application to the Christian in the present moment. Future eschatology was largely personal and treated under the heading of the "four last things"— judgment, heaven, hell and purgatory. Recent thinking on the importance of the future in determining the present and the overall movement of faith toward completion may move us away from fixed and final categories and leave a fair measure of uncertainty as well, but this it would seem is at the very heart of the meaning of faith. Paul's teaching on suffering has, also, important consequences for Christian ethics. In a very real sense, it makes us intimate collaborators in redemption itself.

In the Epistle to the Philippians, written during an imprisonment probably earlier than that of Colossians[1], Paul extols his new-found life in Christ, beside which all else can be reckoned worthless. Here, as elsewhere, Paul lists his credentials stemming from his Jewish background which, by human standards, were unquestionably impressive. Yet they are of no account and he has forfeited them all "in the light of the surpassing knowledge of the Lord Jesus Christ" (3:8). This knowledge which, since his conversion on the Damascus road, is a lived experience, is the source of Paul's justice, one which is wholly gratuitous, not based on law observance. This

---

(1) Discussion about the authorship of a number of Paul's letters, notably Philippians, Colossians and Ephesians, continues, with at least a fair amount of consensus seeing Paul as the author of Philippians and Colossians, with the question of Ephesians being rather more complicated. The author has opted for the Pauline authorship of Philippians and Colossians, finding conclusive arguments to the contrary unconvincing. The date and place of composition for Philippians and Colossians is another matter, on which there is little consensus. We have opted for Colossians composition during the Roman captivity (61-63 A.D.) and Philippians during an earlier imprisonment, possibly at Ephesus (56-57 A.D.). For further discussion of problems of authorship and dates, cf. J. L. McKenzie, **Light on the Epistles**, Chicago, Thomas More Press, 1975.

"knowing Christ" is further specified as rooted in "the power of resurrection" and the "fellowship of his sufferings," the latter transforming him into Christ's death. This reality is the foundation of his hope in final resurrection (3:10f.).

These few verses are a succinct summary of Paul's theology of redemption. The only "gain" Paul knows is that which assures him eternal life. The same can be said of the way it is attained—life in and with Christ. The future (the not yet) is given emphasis as the goal toward which he presses but it is counterbalanced by the present (the already) in which the Christ of the future resurrection is actively experienced. It is an experience, once again with Paul's two moments of death and resurrection, centered in the baptismal commitment. The union with Christ in his resurrection is aptly described as "power"; it is the Spirit-life, which brought Christ himself back from the realm of Sheol and is actively transforming the Christian in his passage from flesh to spirit, the pledge of his own future resurrection. But the inner conformity to Christ, as an ontological reality, extends to his death as well by which Paul is joined in **koinonia** or fellowship to the redemptive sufferings.

If the "power" and life are a daily experience for the Apostle, so too are the "fellowship" and the state of death. The struggles within himself, the struggle of bringing Christ forth in others, the hardships entailed in his missionary endeavors, make his references to sharing in Christ's death much more than simple rhetoric. He tells the Corinthians what the cost of apostleship has been: his own human weakness, hard work, imprisonment, floggings, dangers of travel, hunger, thirst, nakedness, sleepless nights. But through it all, he was never alone; his trials are also Christ's, with that same spirit of love which brought the Master through his own Gethsemane extended to the disciple. What Paul and the Philippians are called to endure, as well as the entire Church, constitutes the total passion of Jesus. In the Christian paradox, he who died once and for all dies daily in the very act of bringing to life the bounties of his historical death.[2]

Paul came out of a tradition which undoubtedly made him aware of the difficult and unresolved questions posed by his forebears on the problem of evil. He recognizes suffering and death as sanctions for wrongdoing; there was too much historical evidence for the "wrath of God" being visited upon wrongdoers for him to do otherwise. He realizes as well that the question of retribution can not be satisfactorily explained solely within the framework of the present life. Paul sees the return of the Lord and final resurrection as the decisive moment for setting accounts straight. He gives scant attention to the state of the just who die before the return of the Lord. In the earlier letters, the return is expected soon; hence the question was not a burning one. In the later writings there is less emphasis on the Parousia's imminence, although it never fades from sight. At most, Paul will speak of the just's interim state as "being with Christ" (Ph 1:23), an anticipation of resurrection glory for which Paul at times expresses a strong desire. The realization of this interim state undoubtedly springs from his knowledge that the life in Christ, once inaugurated, can never be extinguished. Yet his principal hope continues to center around the final resurrection of the just. This is not surprising in view of Paul's strong ecclesial hope. With all our emphasis on personal salvation, we have unfortunately shown too little respect for the Apostle's eschatological focus on the redemption of the Church

---

(2) The Pauline thought on this subject is developed at greater length in B. Ahern's "Fellowship of His Suffering," **Catholic Biblical Quarterly** 22 (1960) 1-32.

as a whole. It is for that final victory that he has given his life, and his joy will not be complete until that hope is realized.

But Paul is not interested in echoing voices from the past on the thorny problem of evil, nor is he preoccupied with sanctions present or future. On the question of the Parousia he states what he has received; his destinaries are not ignorant of this teaching, although their understanding of certain particulars often needs correction. Paul raises a more basic question, reflected also in the Gospels, on the meaning of trial and suffering, quite apart from the question of sanctions. It is here that he makes his contribution. Once he has come to a deeper understanding of what it means to be "in Christ" and penetrated the underlying significance of the baptismal ritual, suffering becomes salvific, redemptive, the agent of an even more intense union with Christ. Paul does not see suffering in other than relative terms, refusing to shroud it in some sort of mystique in and for itself. Man suffers and dies because he is a sinner. But Paul is not about to rest the case there. Death has undergone a transformation as has the suffering which is its prelude; it has become the instrument of victory.

In the light of Christ, the evil consequences of sin have a value that the ancients never imagined as an integral part of the divine plan of reconciliation. The challenge emerges with striking clarity. The Christian is called not only to live a new life, to preach by word and example, to witness to Christ in daily life but, just as importantly, to suffer and to die, not simply in imitation but in union with the Lord. And Christ is not a divine onlooker to this drama or one who compassionately accepts the offering of pain. He is one with the sufferer and that which is endured becomes part of that great offering of filial love which, realized once in history, is always being renewed. Death has lost its sting.

The Genesis tragedy has truly proved to be "a happy fault." The love of God and neighbor has found its noblest expression in the crucified Christ and the suffering Christian.

VII.

THE MYSTERY AND RELIGIOUS INSIGHT

The final book of the New Testament canon is by definition apocalyptic, as its name, "Apocalypse" or "Revelation," indicates. It brings the New Testament to a close in what can be described as a final summing up. The book is attributed to a Christian "servant" known as John (1:1) whose further identity cannot be ascertained with certainty. A strong tradition identifies the author as John the apostle, against which position there cannot be said to be decisive contrary evidence. The problem arises when both Revelation and the Gospel of John are attributed to the same author since the two works have marked theological and literary differences. A growing critical consensus sees the two works as related, with the answer probably lying in the direction of a Johannine school or body of the apostle's disciples who consigned his developing teaching to writing at different times.

The visions conveyed to the seer John remind us of the book of Daniel in their imagery, mode of communication, and symbolism. The personification of evil is not the Seleucid dynasty but pagan Rome. Evidence points to the composition of Revelation toward the end of the reign of Diocletian, between 90 and 96 A.D., whose persecution of the Church evoked once again a strong belief in the imminence of divine judgment. The final victory of God is once more articulated but this time with an important difference. The redemption accomplished in Christ stands at the center of Revelation. It may seem that the victory realized in Christ is contradicted by Revelation, as it picks up the apocalyptic End Time struggle in much the same way as its Old Testament forebears. Has Christ triumphed or has he not?—it is a legitimate question posed by the reader as he reaches the bible's final book. But it is here that we must recall the distinction between present (already) and future (not yet) eschatology. There is no doubt that the Christ of Revelation is the victorious and exalted Lamb (5:6), the triumphant Lion of Judah (5:5). As the Lord of history, he alone can break the seals of the scroll which contains God's plan for history's denouement (5:2ff.). Yet that which had been achieved still lacked its full historical application. The difficulties experienced by Christianity at the hands of Rome at the end of the first century raised again, with even stronger fervor, the hope of apocalyptic termination. The circumstances were not unlike those of Daniel but the presence of the already victorious Lamb of God makes this distinctly Christian apocalyptic.

Contrary to an oft-stated belief, a great part of Revelation's symbolism is readily grasped, with much of its imagery drawn from the Old Testament and earlier Christian writings. But, once again, the significance of the message is not concerned with Christians against Rome but rather with the continuation of the ancient belief of the triumph of good over evil, now made more cogent by the fact of Christ's redemptive activity. The days of the beast (Rome) and the dragon (Satan) are numbered; their extinction has been decreed at the end of a period of familiar eschatological travail: invasion, war, famine, and plague. Through it all the elect of God are spared. The final struggle is the work of God alone, actualized through Christ, presented in battle array

(19:11-21). Rome, the epitome of evil as the fallen prostitute Babylon, is reduced to ashes (ch. 18) as, in contrast, the triumph of God is hymned in the heavenly victory song (19:1-10). The End Time nuptials of the Lamb and his Spouse, the Church or the new Jerusalem, are celebrated with celestial splendor. On this climactic note which gives a final defeat to the long-held sway of evil, the New Testament rests its case.

True, in his death-resurrection Christ has already dealt the death blow. In the order of the spirit, evil is already vanquished; but in the order of the flesh, of time, of daily experience, it constantly seeks to entice others to its chambers of death. It has lost the decisive battle but does not want to suffer that loss alone and even in its vanquished state it continues to play the role of the preying beast until its "time will be accomplished." As the book which closes the New Testament was being penned, Christian hope was strong and indomitable, but Yahweh's opponent, who had made his entrance early in the Bible's opening book, has not yet left the scene. Evil was present in persecution, martyrdom, in sin in its many forms and, to a certain extent, it remained inexplicable.

The Continuing Mystery

The present study has tried to indicate in broad lines the major stages of development within Hebrew and Christian thought on the problem of evil. Yet, with it all, one cannot contest the fact that the mystery remains. Old Testament attempts to penetrate it led to different and at times disconcerting conclusions. While such attempts were unquestionably inspired, they operated within human limitations. None of them failed to cast light on the problem but, as we have repeatedly seen, inadequacies were also present. This process of checks and balances within the biblical text itself serves to high-light its theological pluralism. The inspired books themselves evidence the fact that in understanding a transcendent God and his activity, there is no single answer to important questions; answers are partial and approaches are diverse. Though mystery remained, gains in understanding were made. Suffering has gone beyond an explanation solely in terms of retribution or testing to be integrated positively into the whole process of redemption.

Notwithstanding the ebb and flow of the question in its historical evolution, there is a certain continuity. The connection between sin and death is indelibly stamped on the sacred text. Death's domain includes the plethora of ills to which humanity is subjected. Thus, the "weakness of the flesh" which is reflected in suffering and pain is a constant reminder of the evil of sin. Sin is the antithesis of God, the greatest evil. But how is this to be manifest? Humanly seen, sin is desirable, pleasurable, often hidden; its inherent destructiveness is often not evident. How is it to be unmasked? By its fruits it is known. The many ills of human existence serve to underline that far greater disaster which is the death of the spirit. We may speculate about what meaning suffering and death would have had if sin had never appeared. It seems that the process of decomposition would still have been present, with its attendant ills. However, in Scriptural terms, the question is hypothetical. The fact is that sin is a basic given in the Scriptures; they have little to say about the hypothesis of a sinless state. At most we can say that if man's basic orientation toward God had not been deflected, whatever he might have had to endure in the flesh would have been seen differently and differently ordered. The finality of an act colors particulars; the finality of human existence, clearly seen and recognized, would have given a different meaning to the interlocking elements which converge upon it.

It may be difficult to appreciate the Old Testament's struggle with the problem of retribution or to resist a smile at some of its conclusions. But what we cannot fail to esteem is the faith which is at work. Modern man is at a considerable advantage in being able to posit sanctions beyond the grave. For the greater part of Hebrew history, this was not the case. What was known about the hereafter remained obscure; what was clear was that the future offered no solution to present problems. With life so circumscribed, Old Testament faith, centered in Yahweh's active presence among his people in the here and now, cannot fail to evoke a deep respect. As baffling as the problem of retribution may have been, Yahweh's transcendence and justice remained intact. In desperation, he may have been called to answer for his actions but only because experience was at odds with the deep conviction that the Lord was fair and just.

But is not the recognition of limitations an important corollary of the whole problem of evil? The notion of human limits has to figure prominently in any theodicy. The advances of modern technology have enhanced the idea of human sufficiency. To what extent is God still necessary? In so many ways our understanding of man and his habitat has surpassed that of the biblical authors that it is frequently asked to what extent their concept of God is still functional. But evil is a constant reality. Suffering has been alleviated but it has not vanished. The life span is extended but the inevitability of death is no less certain. If anything, very often because of our progress, we stand before devastation, destruction, and disaster of monumental proportions with the feeling of utter helplessness. Examples are countless. The life of a person of great value is suddenly extinguished; a close friend suffers through an interminable cancer; the child dies in the springtime of life. In war and natural disaster, death counts reach staggering levels. Such events raise many questions, as the biblical evidence testifies. But they are also expressive of finiteness, of circumscribed life. In personally confronting evil and in being unable to explain satisfactorily the "why," we know experientially what limits mean. The inherent demands of logic demand an answer but the answer must be found in something beyond. Call it fate or the forces of nature; it is still an appeal to something which knowledge and experience cannot explain, much less define. The Judeo-Christian tradition appeals to the mystery of God.

No one who has stood at the bedside of a mortally ill friend or held the hand of a bereaved parent can fail to understand the demands that limits impose. The fact that words say nothing makes us fear that our silence may convey insensitivity, which is by no means the case. We are brought face to face with mortality, the transient, the inexplicable, with the limits of human existence. But equally unforgettable in such a moment is the oft-repeated lesson of faith. It is this that makes the worst bearable. Religious resignation is not simply a textbook category; it is a datum of frequent experience. The ability to see the tragic in the light of a living faith is not restricted to a choice few in devotional lives of the saints. Anyone involved in a ministry to the sick remains deeply impressed by its pervading presence. The biblical teaching is verified repeatedly. Rather than diminish faith or call for its rejection, suffering can intensify and strengthen it.

Is this then the only answer to evil? Has the age of Christ's confrontation with the Evil One passed? Are cures and miracles no longer a possibility? Speaking out of a Christian tradition, we believe that cures can and do take place. If the power of evil and natural forces were subject to God in the first century, they remain such in the twentieth. There is ample and well-documented evidence that the miraculous does occur even in modern times. Certain forms of religious renewal in recent years give a prominent place to healings as evident proof of the Spirit's active presence. While recognizing the basic legitimacy of the assertion, such fervor calls for a strong measure of caution. Christian tradition has been very circumspect in the face of miraculous claims, and with good reason. That which is of God will in time commend itself to the believer; as in the New Testament, so today signs and wonders can often be deceptive. But we cannot turn away from that which daily experience makes so evident, and it is the faith of those who are not the recipients of cures. When one visits one of the major shrines of Christianity, the impression that lasts and compels is not that of well-attested cures, or perhaps even the revered apparitions that have sanctified the locale, rather it is the faith of the sick and the thousands who attend them. It may be a cause of concern to some that many of the ill no longer seek a cure as the main object of their prayer; to others it speaks volumes on the presence of the Spirit in a vital faith and is a living commentary on what Paul means by enduring in Christ.

The New Testament, as we have seen, casts a new light on the problem of suffering which has had such a long and uneven history of soul-searching inquiry. In the first place, it has inherited latter-day Judaism's belief in the resurrection. It sees final resurrection as a logical consequence of the immortal life in the Spirit, which is inaugurated in baptism and is the ontological basis of Christian hope. The Christian, once reborn, does not experience death; this new life is a present reality which will endure beyond the grave and will find its ecclesial fulfillment in the total victory of the Parousia. Attempts to describe this future or to depict a resurrected body fall short; they can easily become crass in light of the limitations of concept and language imposed by our earthly existence. Paul realized this, avoided undue speculation, and emphasized the differences of the future rather than its likenesses to the present life. But the future is there. As inexplicable as any human tragedy may be, hope still springs eternal in the human heart. This is not the hope of wishful thinking but the hope rooted in the clearly-stated promise of him who has gone before us and already experiences its fruits.

Secondly, there is consolation in suffering. The unity, real and personal, between Christ and his disciple forges the deepest ties between the two "deaths" and their accompanying trials. If Christ is active and actualizing in the Christian mission in the world and present in the initiatives of his followers, he is equally present in the dedicated endurance of those whose mission is suffering. In many ways, the "why" remains unanswered, as does the "why" of a crucifixion. In fact, it is unflagging endurance in the face of unanswered questions that renders suffering valuable. The Christian suffers in Christ and Christ in the Christian. Christian piety has long spoken of the example of Christ in his passion as a point of reference for the suffering Christian. It has spoken of uniting our sufferings with his in terms of moral identification or of offering our trials to him. But this does not do full justice to Paul's thought. Christ is not an overseer or a presiding high priest ready to receive the offering of the distraught worshipper. He is the Christ still active in casting out the demons and in silencing the storm, not through dramatic gesture but through the quiet agony of extended crucifixion. He suffers in his Body, not because it is forced upon him but because that will of love which binds him to the Father is still at work in his members.

In modern western society where suffering has no value and is abhorred, the unsung heroes of religion are those countless souls who in dedication to the Kingdom and united with its Lord are experiencing the sweat and tears of Gethsemane. Unfortunately, the results cannot be measured; they find no place on the statistician's graph. But they contribute in a singular way to the redemption of the world, a redemption which was realized through a death. The sufferer is immersed in that death, at the same time realizing that he is never abandoned and will never suffer alone.

Thirdly, New Testament redemption is ecclesial; it involves a people. The people-of-God terminology has become firmly fixed in post-conciliar Roman Catholicism, although its implications become evident only by degrees. The God of the Exodus took a people out of slavery and fathered an alliance. The collectivity is dominant and the individual finds his place as part of the community. The New Testament is heir to that tradition. It is for the Church that Christ is handed over in death; in his resurrection he sanctifies his Spouse. Redemption and ultimate deliverance, while certainly addressed to the individual, is never viewed apart from the people of God as a whole.

In short, there is much more concern with "building up the Body" than there is in "saving one's soul"; the latter is achieved through dedication to the former. The same line of reasoning must be applied to the experience of evil. Passion and death were the God-decreed antidote to sin. Being united in the death of Christ has the same implications today. Yet we do not limit ourselves to the personal sins of the sufferer. By reason of the Body of which each Christian is a part, the picture becomes much more extended. Christ suffers in his members and for his members. The mutual relationships of love, about which Paul speaks to the Corinthians, binds the members together in their needs. As in the human body so in the Body of Christ, one member cannot say he has

no need of the other. Hence, when the consequences of
sin are visited on a member so as to be inexplicable in
individual terms, they assume meaning in terms of the
Body. And when borne in the spirit of love for the Christian community, evil becomes productive of good. In its
own way, real but intangible, Christian suffering con-
tributes to the building up of the Body to its perfect
stature.

The Suffering God

When we pass from biblical thought to a metaphysi-
cal knowledge of God, the problem becomes more difficult. If God be the very antithesis of evil, how can it in
any way affect him? How can "imperfection" be lodged
in One who is essentially perfect? What meaning can
pain have for the God of "perpetual felicity"? If God is
by nature changeless, it would seem to be mere metaphor to speak of him in terms of joy and sorrow. The
utter simplicity of God makes it difficult to see how opposites can coincide in the divine nature or how a variety
of attributes can retain their distinctiveness. Yet, the
theological difficulties do not permit us to sidestep the
strong biblical affirmations of God's qualities.

In his important study of the prophets, Abraham
Heschel treats the question of divine pathos, God's experience of passion.[1] He notes that God's transcendence
evoked varied responses in human attempts at description or definition. Greek philosophy begins speculation
in ontological terms; the Ultimate or God is seen principally as Being. Since he is the fullness of being, **actus
purus,** his nature excludes the imperfections of non-
being—contingency, mobility, or change in any form.

---

(1) Heschel, A., **The Prophets,** New York, Jewish Pub. Society, 1962, pp.
247-278.

In traditional Christian terms, apart from the uniqueness of the incarnation, the attribution of human traits to God is metaphorical or, at best, analogous. The Hebrew tradition, on the other hand, does not begin with being but with activity and presence. God is initially conceived in terms of relationships, and relationships imply alteration. The God of Israel is a God who acts, a God of mighty deeds. The Bible does not say how He is, but how He acts. It speaks of His acts of pathos and of His acts in history; it is not as "true being" that God is conceived but as the **semper agens.**[2]

The biblical authors never question Yahweh's transcendence or the fact that his ways are not man's ways. But it would be to falsify their intent to reduce Yahweh's vital concern for his people, which finds expression in anger, joy, suffering, and a variety of passionate responses, to figures of speech or literary attribution. The free and unimposed decision to enter into a relationship with the human community was seen as a real commitment which would inevitably demand a price of God himself. It was unthinkable that he would remain personally untouched by the response or lack of it that his decisive choice was bound to evoke. Anthropomorphism was not an attempt to reduce God to human terms; it was not an impropriety that made him manageable. As human speech about the divine, it had its limitations, but this is not to deny that it is making actual affirmations about God. Pathos, for example, illustrates divine concern which was seen as real in God, not as an apt invention in the interests of moral exhortation. If the Old Testament writers were to be told that such properties cannot be predicated of the perfect Being, then they would be forced to respond that their God was evidently

---

(2) Ibid., p. 264.

less than perfect. The fact is that they would not have
seen such qualities as imperfections. Quite the opposite.
It is their absence that would have been an imperfection.
To substitute the God of the prophets, who could both
delight in his people and punish them in his anger, with
a detached Supreme Being incapable of change in relationships or experience would have meant the imposition
of unwarranted restrictions. Above all, there was the
relationship of love. In the only understanding that the
biblical man had, love meant exposure, risk, intensifica-
tion or rejection. If the lover could not experience these
possibilities, he could hardly be said to be in love.

Hence, when the prophets and biblical authors speak
of God's suffering over his people, or suffering with them,
they do not intend mere metaphor. In fact, the very core
of the prophetic vocation was the sharing by the prophet
in what were seen as the real sentiments of Yahweh.
Divine pathos does not degrade or caricature its subject.
In the biblical books it is marked by a reverent usage.
God may become angry but he is not given to irrasci-
bility. His wrath is justified and transitory; it is his
compassion and mercy that are enduring. Suffering is
never imposed upon him; he suffers because of his chosen
relationship. As we have stated, such a manner of speaking is only a partial utterance about God; it is inadequate
and, at best, an approximation. But it is rooted in the
belief that God is active, vital, and concerned. The Old
Testament is all too aware of the differences between
the Creator and the created, but it is also aware of likenesses, which it is at pains to capture. There was a unity
of conscious acts in God and repeated manifestations
of his will; he was not static, unresponsive or unaffected.
If we are to give the Hebrews' belief its due, then we
must accept its premise: Yahweh is truly a God of concern and for that very reason a God who suffers.

In passing to the New Testament, how are we to see

the suffering of God in the Christ event? Is the Father really affected by the Son's death or does he remain internally detached in view of the prerequisites of the divine nature? Is New Testament soteriology to be seen solely in terms of the suffering endured "in the flesh" by the incarnate Son of God? That the Son suffered as man is an unquestionable datum of revelation but theological inquiry has carried the question further in terms of the divine pathos as extending from the Old Testament to the New. It asks to what extent divinity is itself involved in the God-Man's salvific act. What are the consequences of the self-emptying or **kenosis** of the Philippians' hymn for God himself? the meaning of Christ's cry of abandonment as he suffers?

Early Christianity maintained the human-divine balance in Christ by the doctrine of the two natures. In the single person of Christ both the nature of God and the nature of man are present. The former is incorruptible, unchangeable, absolute, and therefore incapable of suffering and death. In his human nature Christ is heir to all the opposite characteristics, truly a man among men. The distinction between the two natures was scrupulously safeguarded in traditional Christology, allowing, however, for the attributes of both natures to be predicated of the single Person, operative in both. While one could say that the Son of God suffered, it could not be said that the divine nature suffered.

Jürgen Moltmann responsibly confronts the problem of how far it is possible to overcome the distinction between the two natures in understanding Christ's cry of desolation, while respecting the tradition of the Church.[3] Can it be said that God suffers in the Christ event? Moltmann sees the Council of Nicea's teaching

---

(3) Moltmann, J., **The Crucified God**, London, SCM Press, 1973, pp. 227-235.

that God is not changeable in terms of the divine freedom from any form of constraint from without. He is free to communicate himself **ad extra,** and to enter into new relationships. To say the opposite would be to impose restrictions on divine autonomy which are not called for. Thus, unchangeableness would be relative, not absolute.

The same would be true of suffering. Suffering is not necessarily imposed from without, with its only alternative being non-suffering. There can be an active and willed suffering at the service of love. Moltmann asks what meaning the word "love" would have if there were no possibility of suffering. How can there be the total acceptance of another, while remaining internally untouched by the result of such acceptance? Nicea excludes any deficiency in God's being; on this there can be no argument. It is a question of what constitutes deficiency.

If the God of the Old Testament is presented as affected by the action of his people, is it less true of the Father of Jesus? Such Pauline expressions as God's "not sparing his only Son," "handing him over" to death, allowing him to become a "curse for us" should not be robbed of their full implications. It is hardly language applicable to a Father who remains untouched. The point that the prerogatives of divinity must be kept intact is unassailable. At the same time, the extent to which love carried God in the interests of man's reconciliation cannot be diluted. Moltmann proposes a solution in a revitalization of our understanding of the Trinity.[4]

The cross can be understood only in the Trinity and the Trinity in the cross. The point of departure is not nature, but persons. The persons in God are constituted by relationships, and these relationships are determina-

---

(4) **Ibid.,** pp. 235-249.

tive. That is to say, in the light of Christian revelation, God cannot be understood in other than trinitarian terms. The Father, Son and Spirit express an inner relatedness which is fixed in the very nature of God. But, once again, we are confronted with the question: Is it possible to understand relationships, or to speak of them, without using the language of their being experienced, and therefore involving some idea of change? Biblical relationships are only understood in terms of acts, and this is especially true of the act realized in the cross. The Son suffers to the point of godforsakenness, the experienced absence of that central and fundamental Father-Son relationship. The Son suffers this pain of loss as he dies "in the flesh." The Father does not experience the dying but does experience the grief of the death itself. He suffers in the relationship he has as a Father to his Son, which is not the same as that endured by the Son himself. This is not an imposed restriction but the noblest expression of freedom, a freedom of love which joins Father and Son and is itself a relationship, that of the Spirit. Thus, it is not the Son alone who suffers the cost of reconciliation; it is a trinitarian experience embracing the complete Godhead. The closest thing we have to a definition of God in the New Testament is that of love, and it is that love which finds him deeply involved in the event of the cross.

This understanding of divine pathos, advanced by contemporary theology, carries forward the New Testament picture of the God who gave himself up for mankind in his Son. It also complements our study of the problem of evil. If it can be said that God as such is involved in the suffering of redemption, then God is likewise a partner in its continuing effects. These effects are centered in the Christian's fellowship in Christ's sufferings, but they are not detached from the Father's gaze. If he agonized in the loss of his beloved Son, then his sentiments are present still in the continuing trials of his Son's members, who are incorporated into that never-to-be-forgotten death. It is not a question of God being an aloof and distant spectator to tragedy, disaster, and human misfortune, with its meaning known only to him. By reason of the incarnation he is forever a part of it. In freely committing himself in love to mankind, God has become entangled in the human. It is a commitment that reaches to the ugly, the deformed, at times the horrendous, and its price is pain.

Is there a message here as well for those who do not share the vision of Christian faith? The weight of the present study has rested upon the evolving beliefs of the Judeo-Christian tradition, as reflected in its sacred writings. As such, it might be said that its appeal is to a large but still limited audience. There are broader aspects of the problem of evil to which this book has not directed itself as, for example, its meaning in the other great world religions. However, the plan of God as it developed within the history of Israel and Christianity cannot be detached from God's relationship to all of humanity, indeed to creation itself. Nowhere is this more evident than in the incarnation of the Son of God. It is not to a segment of mankind that God gives himself, but he assumes the flesh that is common to all. In so doing, he makes his own the lot, often tragic and sorrowful, to which mankind is heir. In every way, except in sin, he endured that which is common to all, in a way which can fail to inspire only the most hard of heart. In experiencing desolation, abandonment, even the absence of a Father's love, Christ comes closer to the godless and spiritually-bereft than they themselves are wont to consider. In taking human flesh, God has irrevocably committed himself to history and is therefore allied with us in a struggle which still continues. And the love that prompted that daring step is directed toward all.

The mystery remains. Evil continues to taunt us in our haughty modern claims that no problem is insoluble. Philosophy will continue to try to plummet its depth as science will continue to combat its effects. In the meantime the appealing distractions of a cosmetic society will strive to divert our attention from its more somber aspects. But the reality never completely vanishes, often making its appearance anew in starkly brutal terms. Yet one thing is certain. In the light of the cross, the tragic shall never be the same again. Death has been transformed by goodness, generosity, dedication. It is salvific, the major weapon of a battle, the outcome of which has already been determined. There is victory in the air.

How many of the disconsolate through history have made their own the sentiments of the dying Jesus: "My God, my God, why have you forsaken me?" Christ was echoing the twenty-second psalm. It should be remembered that the same psalm in its later verses moves from desolation to confidence and concludes with grateful praise for God's deliverance. Its recitation on Calvary was the prelude to a death that led to glory. To be touched by that death is to know that our ultimate destiny is the same.